ai
weiwei

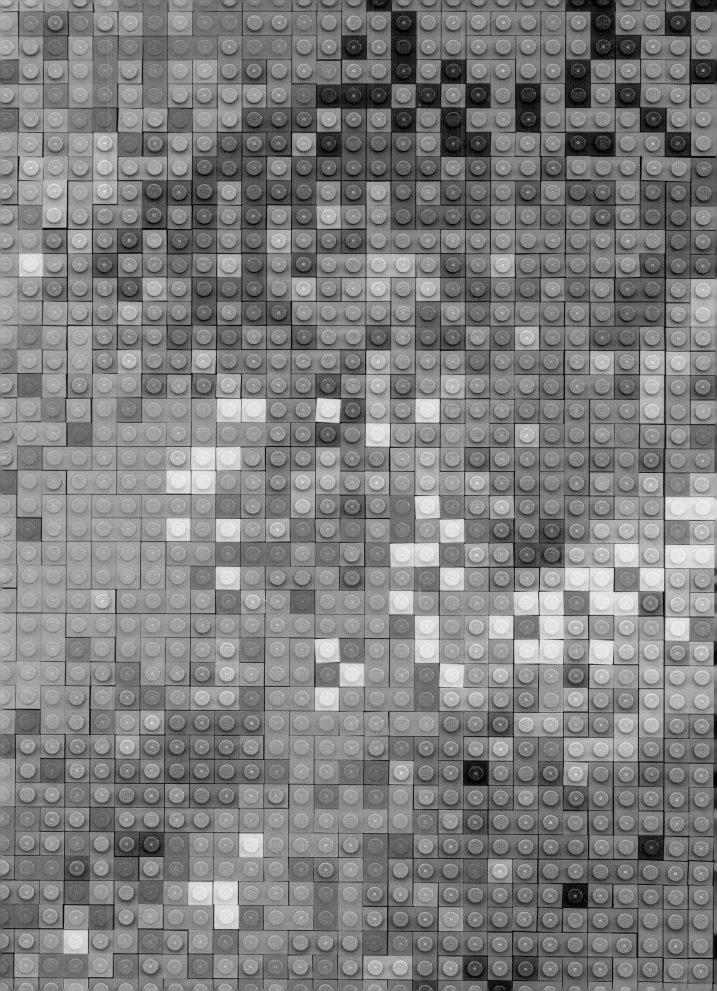

Edited by
Justin McGuirk

Making Sense

aiweiwei

the
**DESIGN
MUSEUM**

CONTENTS

Foreword

Tim Marlow
Director and Chief Executive

In New York, back in 2017, when Ai Weiwei had just finished a remarkable and extensive public art project across the city titled *Good Fences Make Good Neighbors*, I engaged in a public conversation with him at the City University of New York, in front of an audience of predominantly postgraduate artists. New York — Ai described his project there as 'a homecoming of sorts' — was where he had lived, worked, studied and made art from 1981 to 1993. So I began by asking him when he had first realised he wanted to be an artist. 'I still struggle to ask myself that,' he replied. 'Do I really want to be an artist? I'm still undecided.'

There is an element of disingenuous humour here — Ai Weiwei is one of the most important and respected artists in the world — but he remains emphatically self-questioning and self-critical, and he has always adopted an expansive attitude to who he is and what he does. His work takes many forms — aside from sculpture, printmaking, photography and installation, there is writing and film-making. There is also architecture and design, which this exhibition catalogue, *Ai Weiwei: Making Sense*, will showcase. The exhibition will be the first in his career to be framed through that lens of architecture and design. It will span more than 8,000 years of human history from Neolithic tools to digital reproductions, and will include a substantial range of materials from handmade Chinese ceramic cannonballs to machine-produced Lego bricks. It will wrestle with what humans have made and continue to make; how they make; what they choose to keep and what to destroy; and what all this reveals about our changing values socially, culturally, economically and, of course, politically.

Making Sense is not just an exhibition: it is a collaboration between Ai and the Design Museum that quite literally tears down the walls within the exhibition spaces to present a multi-faceted, large-scale installation. It has been led by Justin McGuirk, the chief curator at the Design Museum who, together with assistant curator Rachel Hajek, has enabled Ai's creative vision to inhabit the museum's gallery spaces, its atrium and beyond. It takes a confident and experimentally open-minded curatorial team to let go, where necessary, as well as to give shape to a project — and they have been exemplary in this respect. But the energy and vision, the provocative and questioning spirit that lies at the heart of *Making Sense* belongs to Ai Weiwei, with whom it has been an inspiration to work.

I'd like to thank the Reuben Foundation in particular, whose support for this exhibition has been generous and unflinching. I'd also like to thank Lord Hintze, CQS and all the members of the Ai Weiwei Supporters Circle whose support enhances the collaborative spirit of *Making Sense*. Ai Weiwei's studio team led by Jennifer Ng has been a pleasure to work with, as have Greg Hilty and Courtney Plummer from the Lisson Gallery. Galleria Continua were instrumental in the production of a major new work for this exhibition, *Water Lilies #1*. Above all, though, I'd like to thank Ai Weiwei himself — a man who never stops asking difficult questions about himself, and about us and our place in the world. ○

INTRODUCTION

Justin McGuirk

iPhone Cutout, 2015

A mere flick through this book should establish fairly quickly that while *Ai Weiwei: Making Sense* is being staged at the Design Museum, it does not present the artist as a designer. He has certainly designed buildings – indeed, the architect Wang Shu writes in this volume that he once considered Ai the best architect in China – but the exhibition is not about his architecture either. Rather, it is a meditation on cultural values, and how what we value shifts over time. Design offers the overarching framework. The objects, buildings and landscapes represented have all been designed not just to perform a function but to embody certain cultural values. It is these values that Ai is by turns questioning, challenging or simply attempting to trace. And the visitor is invited to reflect upon them in turn.

The centrepiece of the exhibition is a series of 'fields', each comprising thousands or, indeed, hundreds of thousands of things: stone tools, teapot spouts, porcelain fragments, cannonballs and Lego bricks. Most are remnants of bygone civilisations. They present a highly selective spectrum of making and manufacturing that spans thousands of years – a very brief history of technical progress, if you like. But each field is also a mystery, something that needs first to be configured by our eyes and then made sense of by our minds. What are we looking at? How were they made? How were they gathered here in such profusion? What are we supposed to infer from them? Visitors might feel comforted to know that Ai was equally disoriented by some of these objects when he first encountered them. Here, the works are placed in the context of Ai's documentation of China over the same thirty-year period that he has been collecting. His photographs and films capture a country in the throes of development on a scale that is unmatched in history. The sheer pace and destructiveness of this modernisation is what pushed Ai to start considering and collecting the country's historical artefacts. What cultural values have been lost with all this so-called progress?

Overleaf: Ai Weiwei and his selection of 4,434 stone tools for the Design Museum exhibition (from his collection of 16,134 pieces), 2023

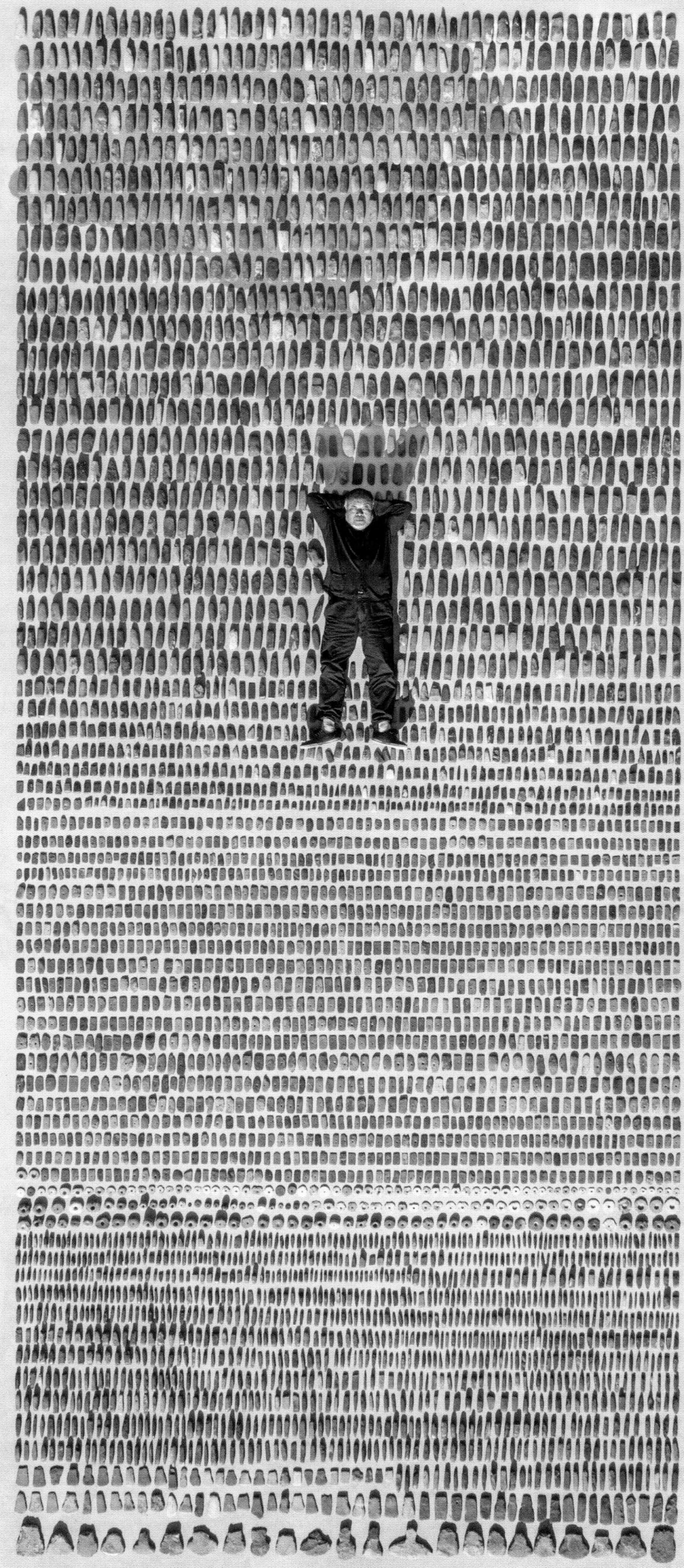

This is the process of *making sense* that gives the exhibition its title. Artist and visitor alike have to make sense of the sheer weight of historical evidence laid out before them. That, in itself, requires a highly active form of looking. But we are also invited to make sense of it against the great storm of change that has reshaped China over the last half-century. The obsession with development has rendered these objects and the histories they represent almost worthless. And then there is another aspect, which is, to invert the phrase, the *sense of making* embodied in the objects themselves. This is where design offers such a revealing lens on cultural artefacts. There are whole histories of making and craftsmanship conjured by the works in the exhibition, each imparting something of the material culture and aesthetic sensibility of their time. The question is: what particular values is Ai in search of?

I sat down recently with Ai at his home outside Lisbon. On the table, he set down the page layouts of this book, on which he had written a series of Chinese characters using a brush and ink. In seeking the best translation of 'making sense', he had realised that it was to be found in the opening line of Laozi's *Dao De Jing*: 'The Dao that can be told is not the eternal Dao.' ● It was the characters for 'that can be told' – in other words, that which can be explained or made sense of – that he latched on to. But Ai was not just arriving at a serendipitous translation. By invoking Laozi at all, he was indicating that design – at least in the form that he appreciates – is not something to be understood through words or reason, but through practice. Good design, in his mind, is arrived at not through logic but through continual effort that ultimately yields revelation. One might think of it as the ten thousand hours often cited as what is required to master an instrument or a craft, at which point one has a certain understanding in one's fingertips.

This, of course, is traditionally more the language of craft than of design. But as Ai points out, there is no Chinese word for design. When he speaks of 'design', Ai is not referring to a largely Western model of practice defined by

the Industrial Revolution, according to which the designer sets out how an object will be mass-manufactured (by other people or indeed machines). Rather, he uses the term loosely to refer to the way things are made in general, and have been made for millennia. As if the definition of 'design' were not loose enough, at least in English, Ai's open-bordered sense of what it means invites a free-spirited discussion about the ways that even ordinary objects embody social and cultural values.

In one of his most famous works, Ai photographed himself dropping a Han dynasty vase, and in that moment established himself as the iconoclastic, middle-finger-flipping artist that people think of today. But even this work should be read less as a statement than as an inquiry into values. Was the vase real or fake? People's reactions varied wildly depending on their perception. And was it Ai desecrating history or was he merely representing the prevailing culture's destructive obliviousness? This exhibition is less interested in questions of authenticity – that theme has been well explored elsewhere – but it has certainly played its part in the development of Ai's public persona. ● His architecture practice in Beijing was called FAKE Design, as if to proclaim his absolute disinterest when it came to authenticity.

However, despite Ai's reputation as a provocateur, this exhibition – and, in particular, the new field works – reveals an artist who, far from dismissing tradition, is in fact highly invested in history. His prodigious collecting of seemingly low-value historical artefacts is nothing if not an inquiry into the kinds of craftsmanship, know-how and aesthetic sensibility that once defined everyday life in China. He is fascinated by how our ancestors used their hands. And while much of what he has collected is essentially detritus, that in no way undermines the power of these objects. For Ai sees design as a language of forms that communicates across the generations. He has spoken of discovering an 'ethical order' in the ancient objects he found in Beijing's flea markets. And this exhibition is his attempt to

● This widely used translation is from Stephen Mitchell's *Tao Te Ching* (New York, NY: HarperCollins, 1988).

● See the exhibition *Ai Weiwei: The Liberty of Doubt* at Kettle's Yard, Cambridge, in 2022.

understand, as well as to contextualise, that ethical order. It is a quest of sorts for values that have been lost, but also a testament to the power of the object as a means of connecting us to different times, different possibilities, different ways of being.

EVIDENCE

In 1993, after twelve years in the United States, Ai returned to China and a Beijing that was in the process of transforming itself. One of his pastimes in those early days was frequenting the flea markets of the city, perusing antiquities. So began three decades of dedicated collecting, not just of fine jade and porcelain, but also of low-value items such as Neolithic stone tools and Song dynasty teapot spouts. With his reputation as an idiosyncratic collector of odds and ends established, people started bringing them to him by the bucketload. Even so, it is extraordinary to encounter the scale of these collections when they are laid out in field works such as *Still Life* (the stone tools) or *Spouts*.

One way to think of them is as evidence: of bygone ways of life, of forgotten know-how and aesthetic sensibilities — evidence of history in general. If that sounds trite, consider how history has been abused in China since the Cultural Revolution, with Mao's doctrine that the past had to be destroyed to build the future. Even the memory of more recent events, such as the 1989 Tiananmen Square massacre, has been methodically worn away. In this context, collecting historical artefacts is a form of rebellion against state-sanctioned accounts, a commitment to preserving the evidence. In her essay (p. 174), Julia Lovell situates Ai Weiwei in a lineage of Chinese scholar—collectors who also sought out an idealised past and used it to challenge the political realities of their day. Ai's interest in Chinese antiquities is no doubt fuelled by his disillusionment with present-day China. But he is clearly hooked as well — hopelessly intrigued by the qualities of these objects, and curious as to the cultures that produced them.

Collecting for Ai Weiwei is not just about acquisition, it is also about research. To see him handling a *bi* (jade disc), one senses that he learns more from touching its surfaces and feeling its weight in his hands than he would from any scholarly treatise. With the less precious items, the cannonballs and broken spouts, he must have known that they would become artworks. But his persistent accumulation of them, without exercising aesthetic judgement or selection, was itself a method. It reflects a commitment to exhaustive knowledge, as if he had to own *all* the spouts to really understand them. In a fascinating conversation with Ai (p. 206), Eyal Weizman refers to the shift in archaeology from the unearthed object itself to the ground around it, where so much other information resides. Ai's field works are so comprehensive that individual objects recede into a continuous ground. Each field is like a geological layer of stone or porcelain craftsmanship. From that single stratum, one has to try to piece together the surrounding civilisation and its ideals.

Amid all this evidence is a history of making. From knapped and rubbed stone tools to fine porcelain to injection-moulded Lego bricks, we are presented with a highly selective chronology of design spanning thousands of years. It is a story of technical progress of sorts, as well as a journey from ancient survival to modern play. We are invited to consider the evolution of forms and techniques. Each field speaks its own language of manufacture. And much of the power of seeing thousands of spouts or tools or cannonballs comes from the tension between the industrial scale on display and the hand labour that produced it. In my essay (p. 198), I propose that the fields are evidence of China's unique technological history, for China had industrial production thousands of years before the Industrial Revolution. It had a very different conception of technology, too, from the Western model that is dominant today. Chinese cosmology held skill and technical tools in harmonious balance, instead of privileging technology itself, and the inevitable de-skilling it engendered with the mechanical and digital revolutions. This may be one reason why Ai Weiwei found an 'ethical order' in the flea-market antiquities. Mysterious to him at first, their qualities of care and hard-won craftsmanship seemed worth understanding and reclaiming.

Study of Perspective, 2022. Installation view

CONSTRUCTION/DESTRUCTION

The backdrop against which the works above are presented is the rapid urbanisation of China over the last three decades. It is often said that between 2011 and 2013, China poured more concrete than the United States did in the entire twentieth century. With unprecedented construction came wholesale destruction. In Beijing, entire neighbourhoods and street patterns, such as the *hutongs* (narrow alleys), were demolished to make way for high rises. One of the first works visitors encounter at the Design Museum is a merchant's house from the Qing dynasty (1644—1911 CE) that Ai acquired before it could be demolished. *Coloured House*, with its new Pop art colour scheme, turns a ghostly silhouette of a vanished past into something luridly upbeat. As with the fields, the trampling of history became not just the context for Ai Weiwei's work, but also yielded his raw materials.

In the early 2000s, Ai began documenting the changing face of Beijing. The *Provisional Landscapes* series of photographs presents a haunting sequence of urban voids. These demolition sites, on land often seized by the state, exist in limbo, awaiting that tide of concrete. Brian Dillon refers to them as a 'desolate version of the picturesque' (p. 190). The architect Wang Shu (p. 184) recalls how, when he invited Ai to teach an architecture studio in 2002, the artist's strategy was to drive the students around Beijing in a bus, having them observe the city in its new reality. That resulted in a series of Warhol-esque films that chart the city's ring roads over hundreds of hours.

Ai was both an active participant in all this construction and a victim of the corresponding destruction. He designed and built major studio complexes in Beijing and Shanghai (the quality of which deeply impressed Wang Shu), only to have them demolished by the Chinese state as punishment for his anti-government activism. One of the field works, *Left Right Studio Material*, consists of the shattered remains of porcelain sculptures that had to be destroyed when one of those studios was demolished. That work in particular speaks

The underground dugout where Ai and his father, Ai Qing, lived when they were in enforced exile in the desert province of Xinjiang during the late 1960s

to Ai's ability to turn destruction into art. But he had already long-since disavowed architecture. His experience of designing the Bird's Nest (Beijing National Stadium) with Herzog & de Meuron, only for it to become the international symbol of an authoritarian state, was too much for him. That refusal to accept architecture's symbolic power runs through the *Study of Perspective* series, in which he flips the finger at iconic landmarks. These are newly presented here as graphic pigment prints that Ai feels better suit the language of design.

Yet more destruction – and more evidence – is to be found in a series of works addressing the Sichuan earthquake of 2008. Thousands of schoolchildren died in the earthquake when schools collapsed because of shoddy construction linked to cost-cutting and corruption. Ai collected some of the warped steel rebar from the wreckage and had it sculpted in marble. Later, he carried out an investigation to establish the names of all the children who had died, and he has most recently commemorated them in the powerful graphic work *Nian Nian Souvenir*, in which the 5,197 names are stamped in red ink using hand-carved jade seals. Tragedy, destruction and injustice are some of the driving forces of Ai's work, and it is through painstaking craftsmanship that they are sublimated into art.

Amid all these rising and crumbling structures, Ai invites us to contemplate an idealised landscape. In a new site-specific work, Ai has created the largest Lego image he has ever undertaken, a fifteen-metre-long reproduction of Monet's *Water Lilies*. Monet's water garden at Giverny was famously not a natural feature but a construct, which he created by turning a brook into a pond. In Ai's version, this liquid paradise is punctured by a doorway, which was the entrance to the underground hovel in the desert province of Xinjiang where he and his father, Ai Qing, lived in exile in the 1960s. This subtle and highly personal intervention seems to subvert the idea that the individual, architect or not, has any agency in the way landscapes or lives turn out.

ORDINARY THINGS

One of the axioms that those who write or think about design often resort to is the notion that 'everything around us has been designed'. This formulation suggests that, while the design canon dwells on a sequence of famous chairs, lamps and devices, the works of design that really influence our lives are all the other things that shape our daily experience in ways we barely notice. The truth, however, is that all those other things remain largely unnoticed even by prominent advocates of design, and it takes an artist to draw our attention to them. A polystyrene takeaway box, for instance, might be seen as simply an unfortunate piece of disposable packaging – an object with a useful life of minutes and an afterlife of decades. But when Ai Weiwei has that takeaway box carved in marble, he is drawing our attention to it as an object supporting the daily existence of millions of Chinese workers. Here it becomes a piece of our actual culture, as opposed to our idealised culture, and a monument to routine experience.

In the spirit of his early influences, Duchamp and Warhol, Ai has for years drawn seemingly inconsequential, mass-produced objects into the gallery context. Coat hangers, sex toys, construction helmets, cosmetics bottles, pieces of foam, handcuffs, toilet roll – each of these Ai has rendered in marble, jade or glass. This is an alchemical process by which a useful but almost worthless object is transformed into a useless but highly precious one. And the true alchemists are the Chinese craftspeople whose skills Ai so respects and is at pains to sustain. Often the choice of object is of personal significance: a coat hanger, for instance, was

Han Dynasty Urn with Coca-Cola Logo, 2014. Installation view

the only possession Ai was allowed when he was in prison. But there are also other reasons he is drawn to them. The panic over toilet paper disappearing from supermarket shelves during the Covid-19 pandemic highlighted the way society depends on the most humble things, unnoticed one day and hoarded the next.

One everyday object that Ai has used to great effect in his own life is an iPhone, with which he documents his every activity and unleashes his views on social media. There is a visual resemblance between the stone tools in *Still Life* and the smartphone that is on the one hand superficial and on the other deeply resonant, connecting the first human tools with the supercomputers we wield in our hands today. One of the works in the exhibition is an iPhone cut out of a jade axe-head. There is an almost ineluctable logic to this piece. Ai is making that correspondence literal and telescoping thousands of years of technical progress into one object.

In an email explaining why he wanted to include a particular work in this exhibition, Ai wrote: 'To define and redefine is the essence of design.' That jade-axe iPhone embodies thousands of years of design iteration, from polished stone to circuitry encased in polished glass. It is redefinition squared. But, to Ai, the axe-head is no less wondrous, and no less a black box, than the smartphone. ○

works

EVIDENCE

'Today, all I can do is pick up the scattered fragments left after the storm and try to piece together a picture, however incomplete it may be.'

Laid out on the floor of the gallery are five 'fields' of objects that Ai has amassed since the 1990s. The function of some of these things is mysterious, and their value questionable. Are they made by hand or machine? Are they priceless or worthless?

When Ai started collecting, China was a nation focused on the future and in thrall to development. History and historical artefacts were often deemed to be of little value. And yet here is the story of thousands of years of human ingenuity. China has a unique history of mass production by hand, and so the impact of some of these fields lies in the fact that they pre-date the machine-led Industrial Revolution. This is the material evidence of bygone civilisations, lost craft skills and forgotten cultural values. In their sheer number, these objects also allude to one of Ai's key themes: the repression of the individual in modern China.

Beijing Photographs, 1993 – 2003
Photographic prints

After twelve years in the United States, Ai returned to
Beijing with a fresh curiosity about Chinese history.
He took tens of thousands of photographs documenting
his new life, which involved visits to Beijing's flea markets
with his brother. Ai also began collecting historical
artefacts, developing a keen interest in traditional Chinese
craftsmanship. This became an obsession that profoundly
changed his value system and influenced his practice.

1   *An antiques shop in Huang Chenggen Park, Beijing,* 1993

2   *Panjiayuan Antiques Market, Beijing,* 1993

3　*Antique vendor, Xi'an*, 1993

4   *Chen Wenji, Ma Xiaoguang, and Xu Bing*, 1993
5   *Ai Weiwei and Zhuang Hui working on White Cover Book, Beijing*, 1995

6   Qin Ga, Ai Weiwei, Sun Yuan, Peng Yu, and Zhu Yu at Ai Weiwei's studio in Caochangdi, Beijing, 2000
6.1   Zheng Guogu, Ai Weiwei's studio in Caochangdi, Beijing, 2000

7 *Ai Weiwei working on* Still Life *in his studio, Caochangdi, Beijing,* 2000

8   *Buddha feet at the Longmen Grottoes, Luoyang*, 1994

9   *The head of a Ming Dynasty warrior sculpture, Ai Weiwei's studio in Caochangdi, Beijing,* 2003
10 *Forbidden City, Beijing,* 1993

11   *June 1994, Beijing*, 1994
12   *Lu Qing and poster, Beijing*, 1994

13 *Soldier on sentry duty, Tiananmen Square, Beijing,* 1994

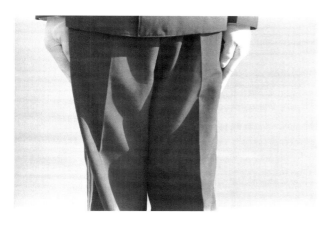

15   *Ai Weiwei smashing a Han Dynasty urn, Dongsi Shisantiao, Beijing,* 1995

16   *Ai Weiwei smashing Qing Dynasty porcelain, Dongsi Shisantiao, Beijing*, 1995

17   *Ai Weiwei working on Whitewash in his studio, Caochangdi, Beijing,* 2000

18   *He Yunchang models for Arm, Ai Weiwei's studio in Caochangdi, Beijing*, 2000

19–21   *Carpenters at work, Ai Weiwei's studio in Longzhuashu, Beijing,* 1997

22 *Carpenters at work, Ai Weiwei's studio in Longzhuashu, Beijing,* 1997

Still Life, 1993 – 2000
Stone, installation, dimensions variable

The tools in this field date from the late Stone Age. The
axe-heads, chisels, knives and spindle whorls remind us
that the origins of design are rooted in survival. Any one
of these could be a museum exhibit, and yet Ai found them
cheaply available in flea markets. In laying more than
4,000 of them side by side, he challenges our view of them
as rare finds. Instead, he treats them as ordinary things,
like a geological layer of forgotten history.

Following spreads
Detail and installation views

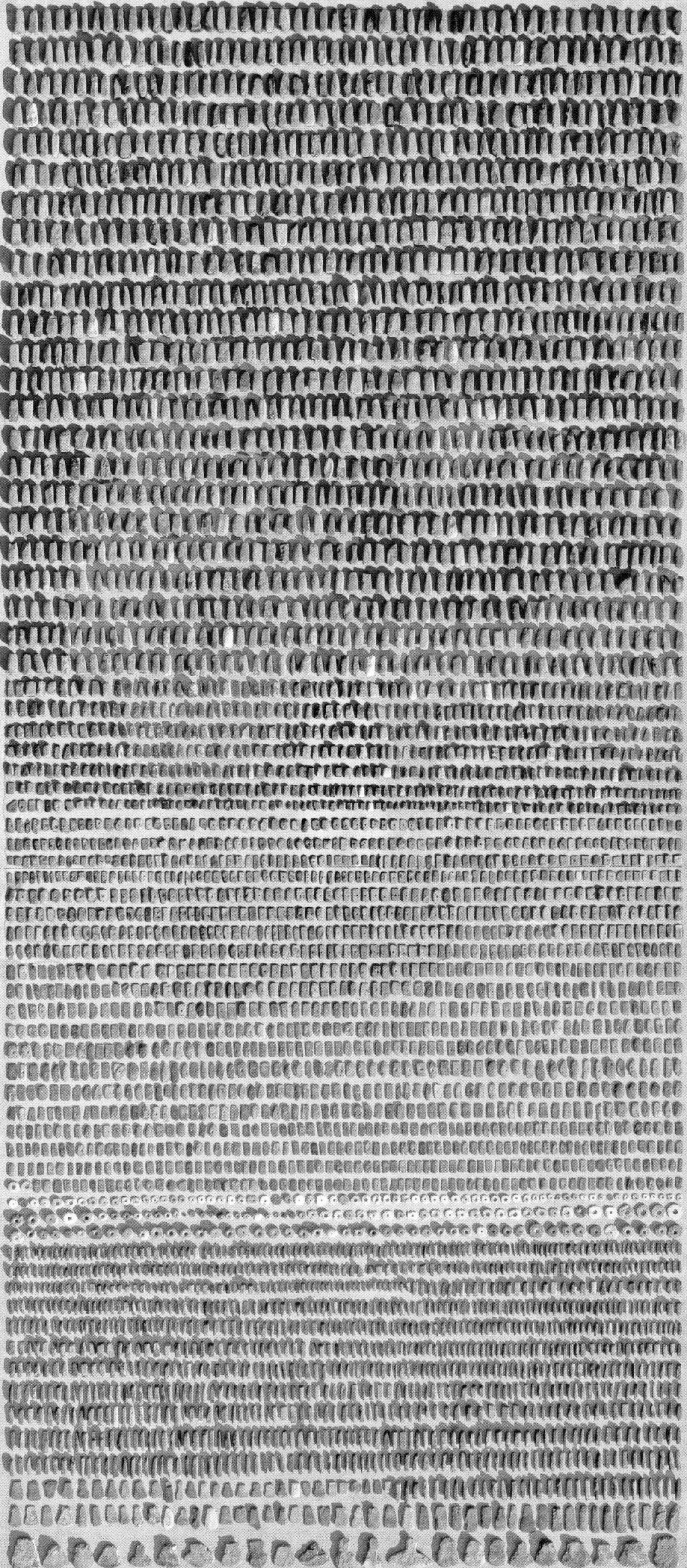

iPhone Cutout, 2015
Jade, 11.5 × 5.8 × 0.9 cm
Courtesy of Mao Ran

An iPhone has been cut out of a jade hand-axe from the
Neolithic era. The implication is that modern technology
is rooted in our early craft know-how. Yet there are jade
knives in Ai's collection that no one knows how to make
any longer, suggesting that humans don't only gain
technical knowledge but also lose it.

iPhone 4 (Jade), 2015
Jade, 11.5 × 5.8 × 0.9 cm

Jade Axe, Neolithic era
Jade, 15 × 6 × 1 cm
Courtesy of Li Dongxu

Jade Adze, Neolithic era
Jade, 19 × 6.5 × 1 cm

Spouts, 2015
Porcelain, installation, dimensions variable

Ai has collected hundreds of thousands of porcelain spouts
from teapots and wine ewers crafted by hand during the
Song dynasty (960–1279 CE). If a pot was not perfect when
it was made, the spout was broken off. That quantity, of
which 250,000 are laid out here, attests to the scale of
porcelain production in China even a thousand years ago.
Ai is also offering a commentary on freedom of speech,
with the spouts – or mouths – having been removed.

Following spreads
Detail and installation views

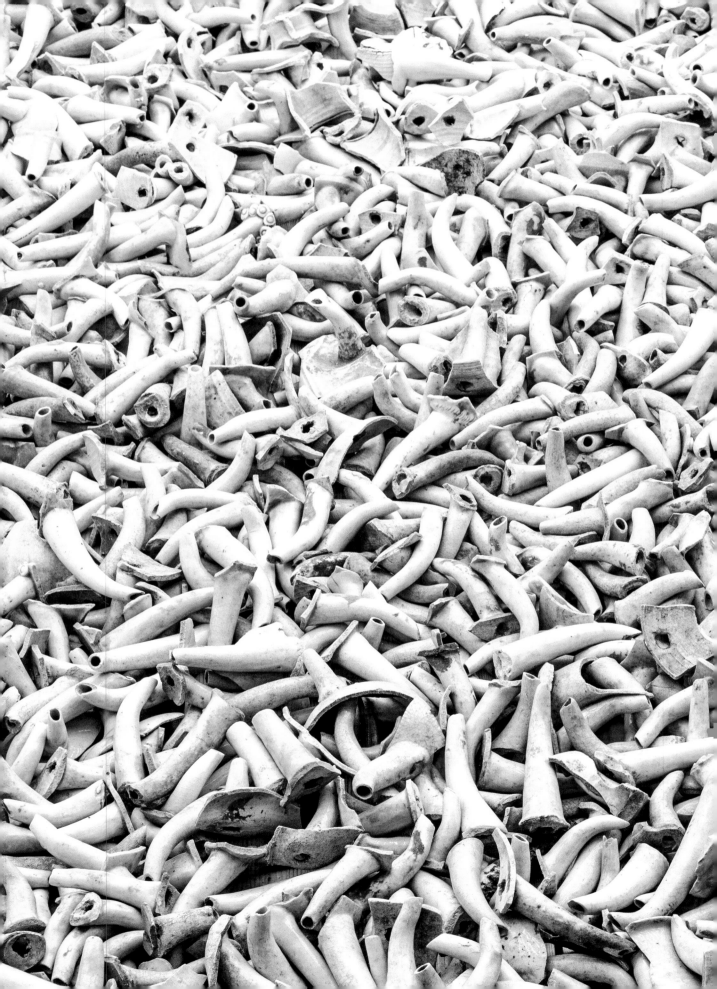

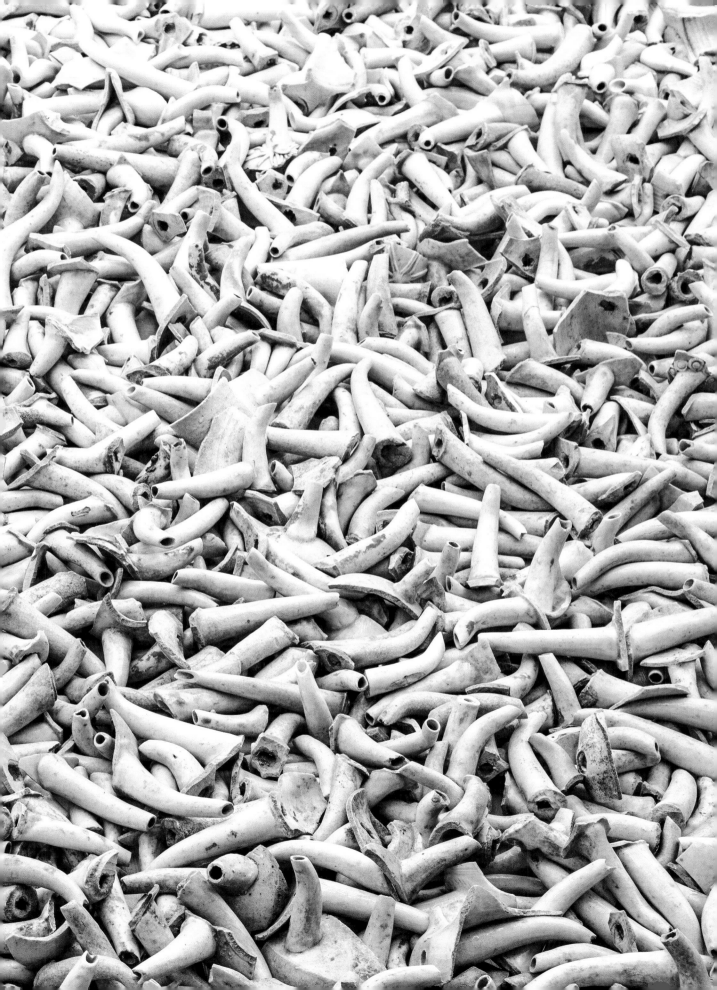

Untitled (Re-firing Spouts from the Song Dynasty), 2015
Porcelain, dimensions variable

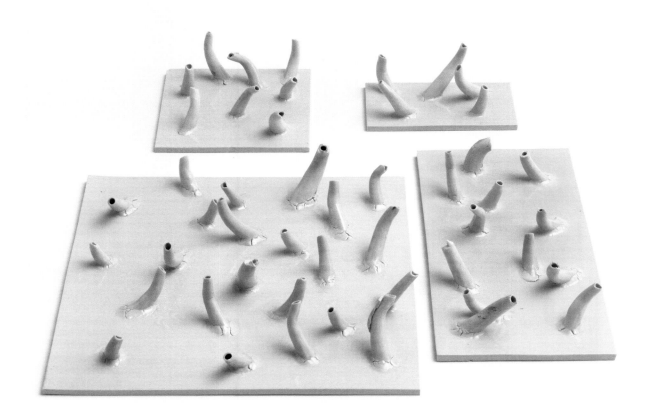

Handled Ewer, Song dynasty
Porcelain, 14 × 13 × 9 cm

Remains, 2015
Porcelain, set of thirteen, dimensions variable

Porcelain is well known to be precious and fragile.
Remains is a reminder that these qualities also apply
to life itself. The porcelain bones here are replicas of
human bones excavated at a labour camp in operation
in the late 1950s under Chinese leader Mao Zedong.
Thousands of intellectuals — including Ai's father, the
poet Ai Qing — were exiled or killed during the purges
of this period.

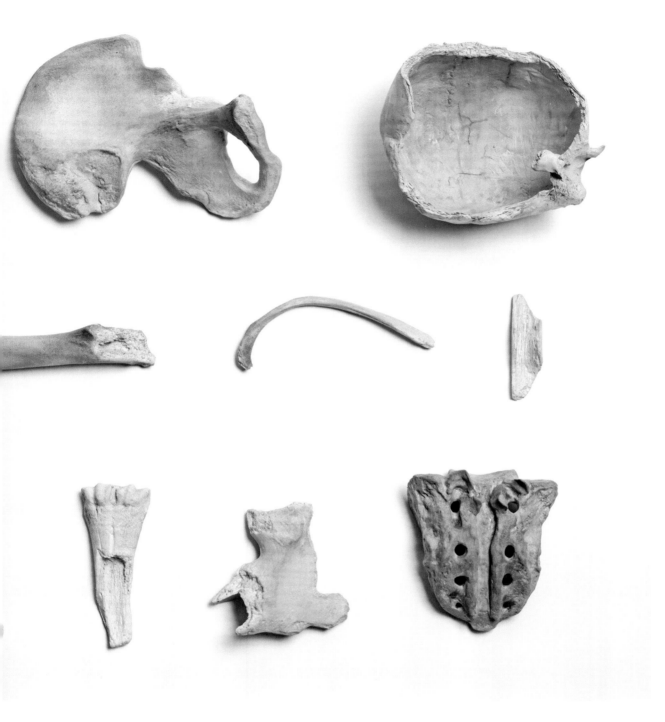

Untitled (Porcelain Balls), 2022
Porcelain, installation, dimensions variable

When Ai first encountered these balls, he had no idea what
they were. It turned out that they are cannonballs made
during the Song dynasty (960–1279 CE) from Xing ware,
a high-quality porcelain. Ai was struck by the fact that this
precious and seemingly delicate material was once used for
weapons of war. There are more than 200,000 here, which
makes it hard to comprehend that they were handmade.

Following spreads
Detail and installation views

Left Right Studio Material, 2018
Porcelain, installation, dimensions variable

In 2018, Ai's 'Left Right' studio in Beijing was demolished
by the Chinese state. These fragments are the remains of
his porcelain sculptures that had to be destroyed as a
result. One of the complete sculptures, *Bubble*, can be
found on page 76. The remains are a form of evidence of
the repression that Ai had suffered at the hands of the
Chinese government, as well as a testament to his ability
to turn destruction into art.

Following spreads
Detail and installation views

Bubble, 2008
Installation view at Ai Weiwei's Left Right studio in Beijing

Untitled (LEGO Incident), 2014
Lego bricks, installation, dimensions variable

As a modular building system, Lego is a good metaphor for
the speed and repetitiveness of much recent construction
in China. Like other objects in Ai's fields, it is produced
on an industrial scale, though machine-made as opposed
to handcrafted. Ai started working with this material in
2014 to produce portraits of political prisoners. When Lego
briefly stopped selling to him as a result, his response on
social media led to overwhelming donations of bricks from
the public. Ai often uses Lego to construct images because
it is an objective kit of parts that removes the trace of the
artist's hand and does not rely on his skill or taste.

Following spreads
Detail and installation views

CONSTRUCTION
/DESTRUCTION

'I was also recording the demolitions, the perpetual upheavals and ruinations that accompanied the urbanisation process … I began to see these acts of documentation as essential to my life not only as an artist but as a citizen.'

In the last two decades, China has witnessed a pace of urban expansion never seen before. With rapid construction came mass destruction, as historical urban fabric was erased to make way for new development. Ai himself has been both a beneficiary and a victim of this cycle. He has designed dozens of buildings, including his own studio complexes in Beijing and Shanghai. Both studios were destroyed by the state as punishment for Ai's political activism. The works in this section provide the context for Ai's continual questioning of value. He has documented the changing face of Beijing through photographs and video. At the same time, he has acquired temples and houses that would have been demolished — not to preserve these structures but to present them as reconfigured ruins that suggest a world in flux. Ai invites us to ask how prevailing value systems construct the world, and in turn to imagine what landscapes we desire.

Through, 2007−8
Wood, 5.5 × 13.8 × 8.5 m
Courtesy of Lisson Gallery

Through combines the columns of a Qing dynasty
(1644−1911 CE) temple with tables from the same period,
bringing architecture and furniture together in a complex
structure. In Chinese, furniture-making is known as 'small
carpentry' and architecture as 'big carpentry'. Here, the two
are merged. Destruction is the starting point of something
more constructive: a ruin becomes a new ensemble.

Water Lilies #1, 2022
Lego bricks, 2.7 × 15.3 × 0.1 m

The largest Lego work Ai has ever created, this is a
recreation of one the most famous paintings by French
Impressionist Claude Monet. We think of the painting
as a portrait of nature, but Monet's lily pond at Giverny
was a construct – an idealised landscape that he himself
designed. To the right of Ai's version is a dark portal, which
is the door to the underground dugout in Xinjiang province
where Ai and his father, Ai Qing, lived in forced exile in
the 1960s. Their hellish desert home punctures the watery
paradise. The image has been constructed out of Lego
bricks to strip away Monet's brushstrokes in favour of
a depersonalised language of industrial parts and colours.

Following spread
Detail view

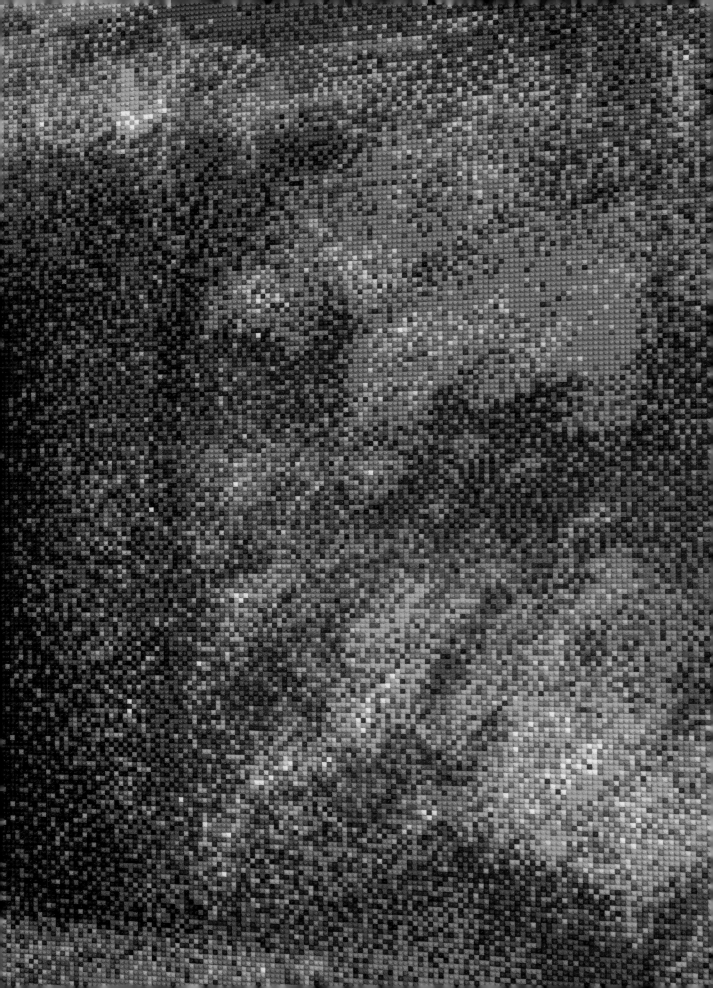

Cabinet, 2014
Wood, 240 × 160 × 100 cm

Crafted from a hardwood traditionally used for the finest
furniture, *Cabinet* memorialises a tragedy. In 2012, five
boys in Guizhou province in southwest China took shelter
from the cold in a rubbish container, lit a fire and died
of carbon monoxide poisoning. Ai's sculpture replicates
that container.

Rebar and Case, 2012
Wood, marble, foam, dimensions variable

More than 90,000 people died in the 2008 earthquake in
China's Sichuan province. Ai was deeply affected by the
fact that many were children trapped in collapsing school
buildings. The sub-standard construction of these buildings
was likely linked to corruption. From the rubble, Ai took
some of the twisted steel rebar used to reinforce the concrete
and had replicas made in marble. Here, they have become
commemorative sculptures on coffin-like plinths.

Backpack Snake, 2008
Backpacks, 0.7 × 17 × 0.4 m

This sculpture is among several works dedicated to the
victims of the 2008 Sichuan earthquake in China. It is
assembled from schoolchildren's rucksacks, recalling those
which Ai had encountered buried amidst the rubble when
he visited the epicentre.

Life Vest Snake, 2019
Life vests, 0.9 × 22.5 × 0.7 m

These vests were collected from the shores of Lesbos,
Greece. Seemingly unremarkable on their own, they are
used here to emphasise society's most disempowered.
The victims of the refugee crisis in Europe are the focus
of this sculpture, which urges us to be more empathetic.

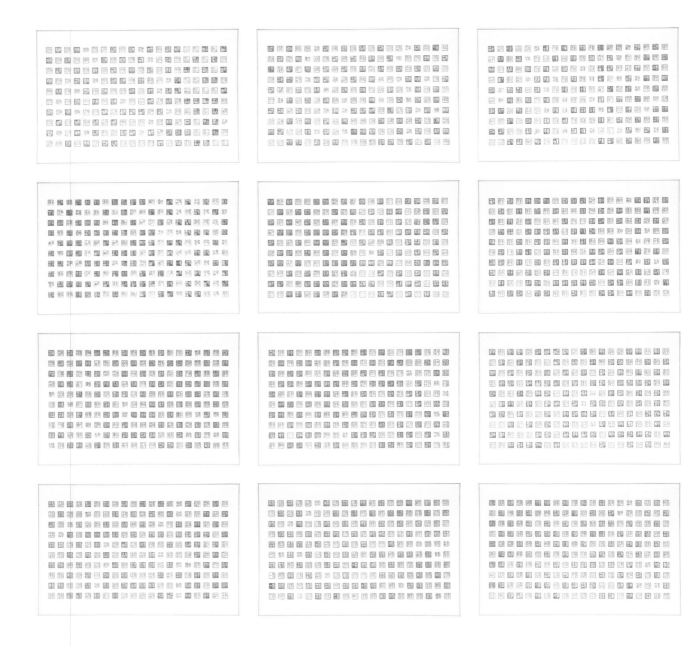

Nian Nian Souvenir, 2021
Ink, paper, set of twenty-six, each 45 × 66 cm

To Ai, the significance of design often lies in its potential
to give form to our memories and experiences. *Nian Nian
Souvenir* is a graphic monument, bearing the names of
the 5,197 schoolchildren who died in the 2008 Sichuan
earthquake. Ai identified them by organising a volunteer-
led investigation. Each name has been stamped in an
ancient script, using a hand-carved jade seal. An example
of one of the *Nian Nian Souvenir* seals can be found on
page 107.

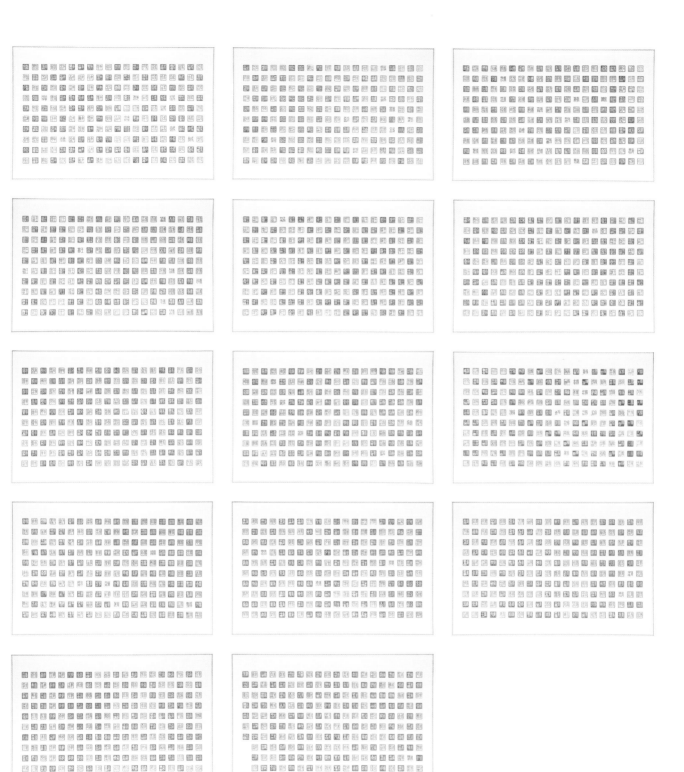

Following spread
Detail view

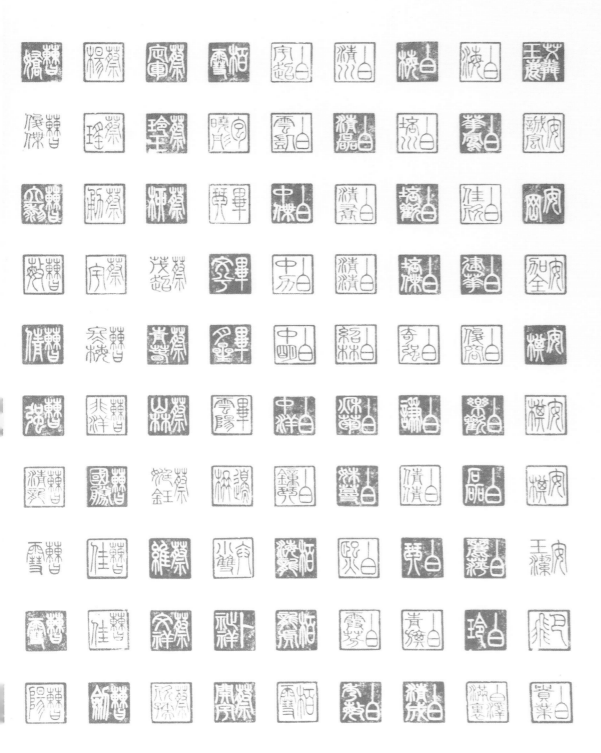

Nian Nian Souvenir seals, 2021
Jade, wood, each box 7.4 × 44.5 × 24 cm

One of the *Nian Nian Souvenir* seals, 2021
Jade, each 4 × 2 × 2 cm

Provisional Landscapes, 2002—8
Photographic prints, each 70 × 88.3 cm

These photographs capture the empty spaces left by
demolitions as Chinese cities underwent an unprecedented
wave of development in the 2000s. Ai photographed
hundreds of void spaces as evidence of the erasure of the
urban fabric in the name of progress. But Ai was also
documenting the aftermath of the often-violent process
by which the state confiscated land from landowners in
its pursuit of high-speed economic growth.

Beijing 2003, 2003
Video, 150 hours

The early 2000s were a period of intense development
in Beijing. When Ai was invited to teach an architecture
course at Beijing's Tsinghua University, he asked his
students to look at the way the city was changing. They
rented a bus and filmed for sixteen days as they drove
through every *hutong* (narrow alley) and street. The result
is a monumental record of a city that has since vanished.

Chang'an Boulevard, 2004
Video, 10 hours 13 minutes

Beijing: The Second Ring, 2005
Video, 1 hour 6 minutes

Beijing: The Third Ring, 2005
Video, 1 hour 50 minutes

National Stadium, 2005–7
Photographic prints, each 91 × 111 cm (framed)

In the build-up to the Beijing Olympics in 2008, the
National Stadium became the symbol of a newly powerful
China. Ai worked on the design of the Bird's Nest, as it
became known, with the Swiss architects Herzog & de
Meuron. He photographed the construction of this
monumental structure to capture the labour of the tens
of thousands of largely rural migrant workers. Ai later
distanced himself from the stadium, not wishing to
become a tool of government propaganda.

Study of Perspective, 2022
Pigment prints, canvas, set of twelve, 102 × 136 cm

Power, as embodied by culturally and politically significant
sites, is Ai's target in this longstanding series. He repeatedly
performs a scornful gesture, subverting the traditional
artistic method for measuring perspective. In doing so,
he rejects the expectation that these institutions should
be respected or revered. Begun in 1995 as a series of
photographs, these have been turned into pigment prints,
using what Ai sees as the more graphic language of design.

Top   *Tiananmen Square, Beijing, China*
Bottom *The White House, Washington, D.C., USA*

Top   *Victoria Harbour, Hong Kong*
Bottom   *St Mark's Basilica, Venice, Italy*

Top   *Eiffel Tower, Paris, France*
Bottom   *Mona Lisa, Louvre, Paris, France*

Top   *Metropolitan Museum of Art, New York, USA*
Bottom   *Reichstag, Berlin, Germany*

Top   *Colosseum, Rome, Italy*
Bottom   *Houses of Parliament, London, UK*

Top   *Bern, Switzerland*
Bottom   *Trump Tower, New York, USA*

Coloured House, 2013
Wood, 7.7 × 6.2 × 10.25 m

This house once belonged to a prosperous family in Zhejiang
province, in eastern China, during the early Qing dynasty
(1644–1911 CE). It is made entirely of timber, using a
traditional post-and-beam system. Most houses of this
period have been demolished, giving this structure a ghostly
quality. Ai has painted the house with industrial colours,
combining ancient and modern, and installed it on crystal
bases – giving presence and status to this unlikely survivor.

Following spreads
Detail and installation views

ORDINARY THINGS

'By changing the meaning of the object, shaking its foundations, we are also changing our own condition. We can question what we are.'

Ai has always worked with found objects — ordinary, often disposable things, made of plastic or polystyrene, that embody the most everyday and invisible kind of design. Using precious materials, Ai then transforms something useful but worthless into something useless but valuable. In forcing our attention on to the easily overlooked, he asks us to assess its value. Is a takeaway container carved in marble a critique of consumer society, or a monument to the daily lives of millions of people? The tension that animates these works is between the cheap, mass-produced object and the highly skilled craftsmanship that turns it into art. Ai works with traditional Chinese craftspeople — masters of jade, porcelain and marble — and seeks to keep their centuries-old skills alive. Elevating everyday objects into artworks, Ai brings past and present together.

Hanging Man, 2009
Wood, steel, each 3.8 × 40 × 45.1 cm

This homage to Marcel Duchamp turns a coat hanger
into the French artist's profile. Ai has credited Duchamp
as one of his greatest influences. Duchamp's pioneering
use of manufactured objects as 'ready-made' art — and his
witty subversion of an object's function and meaning —
are echoed in many of the works in this exhibition.

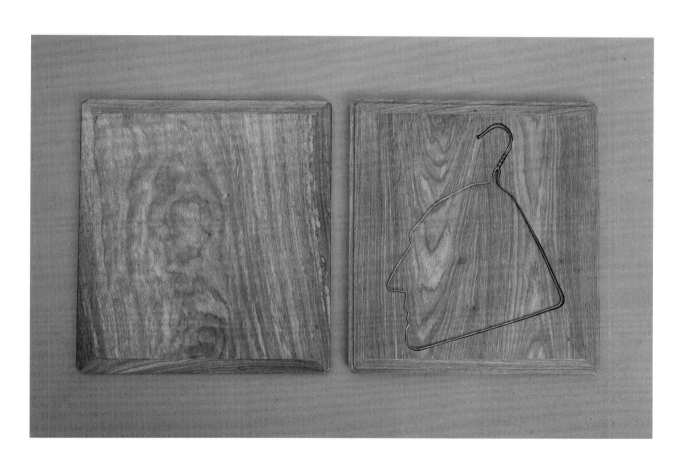

Glass Helmet, 2022
Glass, 15 × 28.5 × 21 cm

A worker's hard hat cast in glass becomes at once strong
and fragile. Ai disrupts our expectations and draws our
attention to miners and workers who have died in labour-
related accidents.

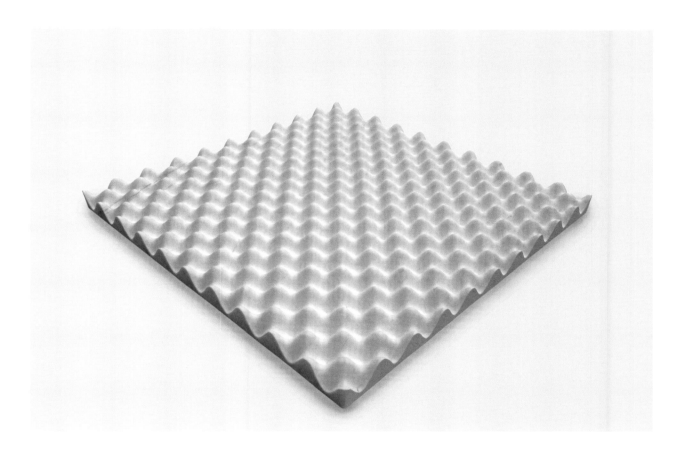

Marble Foam, 2018
Marble, 4 × 65 × 65 cm

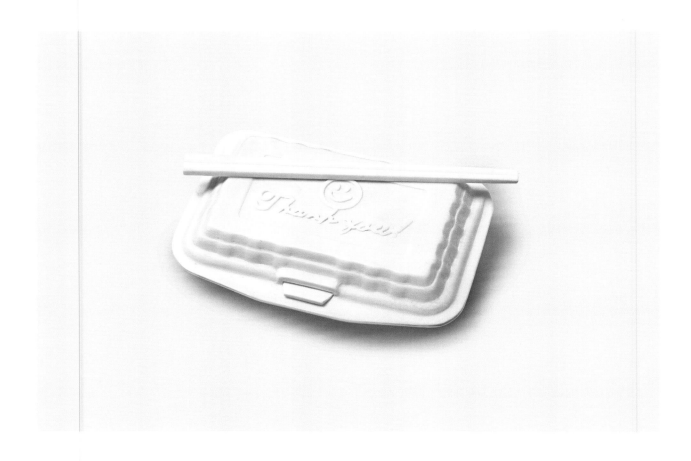

Marble Takeout Box, 2015
Marble, 5 × 18 × 13 cm

Humanity's desire for convenience has given rise to hyper-
disposable objects. A styrofoam takeaway box is a throwaway
item, but carved in marble it becomes a monument to the
daily lived experience of millions of workers.

Glass Toilet Paper, 2022
Glass, 13.5 × 14 × 14 cm

Our dependency on humble things is only exposed when
they become scarce. This was the case with toilet paper
during the Covid-19 pandemic. Glass is used in this work
as a metaphor for the fragility of society itself.

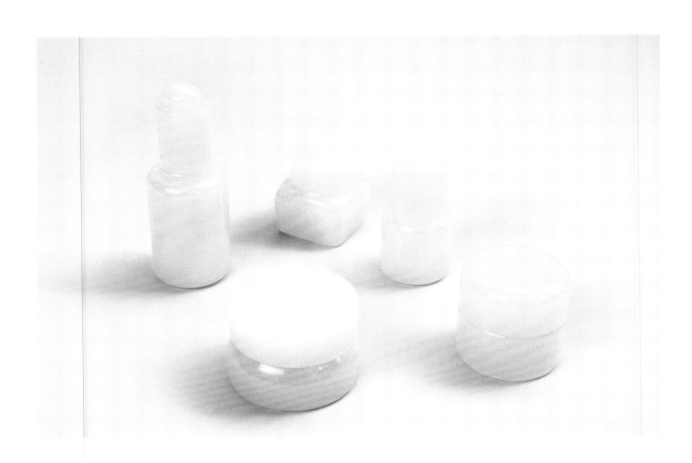

Cosmetics, 2013
Jade, set of five, dimensions variable

Sex Toy, 2014
Jade, 2.7 × 31 × 7.5 cm

Hanger, 2011
Wood, 0.8 × 50 × 24.5 cm

Hanger, 2012
Stainless steel, 1 × 48 × 22 cm

Hanger, 2013
Crystal glass, 0.9 × 51 × 23 cm

An everyday plastic hanger, rendered in different materials,
becomes sculptural or unexpectedly refined. The hanger is
a symbolic object for Ai as it was one of the few possessions
he was permitted to have during his secret detention by the
Chinese authorities for eighty-one days in 2011.

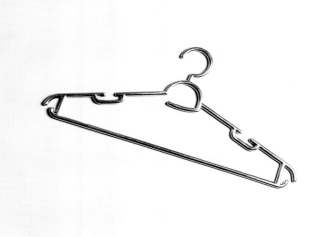

Handcuffs, 2011
Jade, 9 × 30 × 1.5 cm

Themes of free speech, incarceration and surveillance
permeate Ai's work, these handcuffs being one example.
He subverts them as a symbol of oppression by carving
them in jade, a material believed to have protective
qualities in China.

Handcuffs, 2015
Wood, 2.5 × 40 × 13 cm

Han Dynasty Urn with Coca-Cola Logo, 2014
Earthenware, paint, 28 × 27 × 19 cm

Is Ai trying to shock us by painting a modern corporate logo
on a Han dynasty (206 BCE–220 CE) urn, or is he asking
us to reflect on the cultures that each of these represents?
In bringing them together, Ai collides two opposing value
systems: one embodying ancient craftsmanship, and the
other a symbol of global consumerism perpetuated through
mass-produced branding.

The Animal That Looks Like a Llama
But is Really an Alpaca 2023, 2023
Wallpaper, dimensions variable

Following spread
Installation view

Marble Sofa, 2011
Marble, each 85 × 92 × 95 cm

Following spread
Installation view

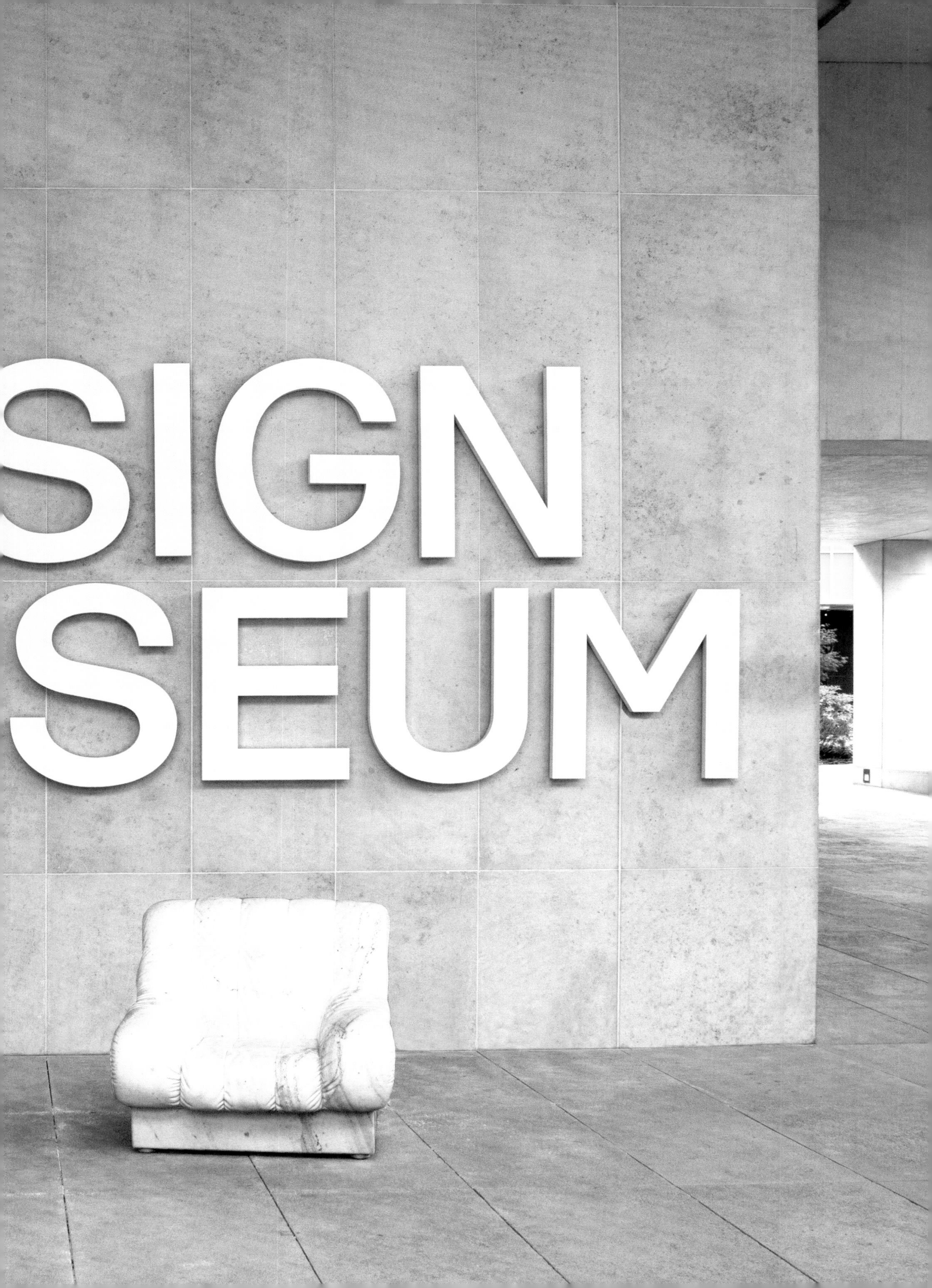
SIGN
SEUM

Pendant (Toilet Paper), 2021
Marble, 160 × 160 × 160 cm

Toilet paper — a seemingly worthless item — was suddenly
sought after when it became scarce during the Covid-19
pandemic. Ai was particularly struck by this because toilet
paper was a luxury when he was growing up in China.
By carving this roll in marble on this grand scale, he
memorialises a moment when we were forced to recognise
the value of ordinary things.

Following spread
Installation view

TEXTS

BEIJING PHOTOGRAPHS

Rachel Hajek

Ai Weiwei working on *Whitewash* in his studio, Caochangdi, Beijing, 2000

The scale at which Ai Weiwei operates is often monumental. And yet, to be custodian of vast inventories of objects, as he is, also demands microscopic attention to detail. Throughout his lifetime, Ai has collected hundreds of thousands of artefacts, and taken almost as many photographs. Where the former represent the echoes of lives that have gone before, the latter trace the unfolding of Ai's own personal history.

Returning to China in 1993 at the age of thirty-six, having lived in the United States for twelve years, Ai steadfastly began recording his new life. He captured diverse subjects, ranging from the declining health of his father (the poet Ai Qing) to his wide community of collaborators, and the cats and dogs roaming his studios. ● Ai amassed a trove of 40,000 or so images, spanning a decade. This vast body of work became known collectively as *Beijing Photographs*. The twenty-two photographs selected for this exhibition (found on pages 23–43) demonstrate how Ai's ideas on design and cultural value – the central

theme of the show – began to take shape in this critical period of his life. ● They are a visual archive of a formative decade in his practice.

○

Beijing Photographs documents Ai's nascent obsession with China's material history. He began studying and accumulating artefacts and antiquities in the early 1990s. Collecting has become one of his primary modes of artistic inquiry, and a means through which Ai seeks to make sense of humanity, society and himself. These relics also shaped his exploration of value. Not long after his return to China, Ai spent countless hours frequenting markets with his brother Ai Dan, who was known for his connoisseurship and eye for quality. Plates 1 and 2 are visual evidence of their expeditions to Huang Chenggen Park and Panjiayuan: we see large quantities of wares arranged in informal displays, and mysterious altercations taking place

● For an in-depth publication on the series, see Ai Weiwei, John Tancock and Stephanie H. Tung, *Ai Weiwei: Beijing Photographs, 1993–2003* (Cambridge, MA: MIT Press, 2018).

● The selection was made predominantly from the 613 photographs originally published in *Ai Weiwei: Beijing Photographs, 1993–2003*.

between marketgoers. Travelling a thousand or so kilometres to Xi'an, Ai encounters a weary trader selling Han dynasty urns (Plate 3). The young man's pose suggests his indifference and, in this moment, neither their financial nor cultural worth appear to be particularly high.

It was in this atmosphere that Ai developed his expertise in jade, stone tools, wood and vessels from different dynasties, and began to form his own collections. Other photographs emphasise the contrast between the attitudes held towards these objects by him and his friends (many of them also artists) and by the vendors. *Chen Wenji, Ma Xiaoguang and Xu Bing* (Plate 4), taken at Ai's family residence in Dongsi Shisantiao, shows how he lived alongside these acquisitions, incorporating them into intimate spaces as part of his everyday life. Urns, vases and beads fill the background of the image. Similarly, statues and carvings are carefully arranged and displayed in *Ai Weiwei and Zhuang Hui working on 'White Cover Book'* (Plate 5). The book is significant, too: co-edited by Ai and published in 1995 for a Chinese readership, it was the second of three volumes that aimed to chronicle contemporary artistic developments in China and to disseminate information about Western art-historical discourse. In his memoir, Ai writes that, in China, underground art's 'main component was [often] simply the recording of it'. ● The act of creating a written account of artistic activity that had hitherto gone undocumented was itself a powerful form of resistance. In collecting this body of 'evidence', Ai and his allies gave legitimacy to a radical artistic movement whose very existence had been otherwise discouraged, marginalised or suppressed.

In Plate 6, we glimpse a fraction of Ai's collection of Neolithic stone axe-heads, as they are admired by guests at Caochangdi, the first studio he designed and built, along the outskirts of Beijing in 1999. These relics from bygone makers are handled with the utmost care and are seen

again on a larger scale in *Ai Weiwei working on* Still Life *in his studio, Caochangdi* (Plate 7), where each tool is shown being painstakingly catalogued. This reverence for objects can be read in dialogue with a photograph like *Buddha feet at the Longmen Grottoes, Luoyang* (Plate 8), taken in 1994 when Ai visited the ancient archaeological site. ● Ai's camera alights on these uncanny feet, presumably separated forcibly from the rest of a body, his gaze gravitating towards what others may have judged to be of little significance. Over the centuries, waves of vandalism and looting have destroyed parts of the sculptures. Ai is as invested in documenting, through visual record, the fragments of this history as he is in the surviving complete works of art. Susan Sontag's view of photography as a means of 'uncovering a hidden truth, conserving a vanishing past' is one perhaps shared by Ai. ● Each image in *Beijing Photographs* is a form of deep investigation, presented here as evidence of human activity that reveals how meaning is determined or constructed. In this sense, the photographic series itself – along with subsequent works, such as *Study of Perspective* (1995–), *Provisional Landscapes* (2002–8) and *National Stadium* (2005–7) – forms a continuation of Ai's longstanding collecting practice.

○

In his memoir, Ai writes that 'little acts of mischief in 1994 marked a starting point in my re-engagement with the making of art.' ● A group of images from *Beijing Photographs* attest to this re-engagement, showing the varied approaches Ai takes to making, which is one of this exhibition's key themes. Specifically, the quote speaks to Ai's interest and skill in creating work that questions or disrupts the status quo through simple and subversive gestures. *June 1994* (Plate 11) is one such

● Ai Weiwei, *1000 Years of Joys and Sorrows: A Memoir*, trans. Allen H. Barr (London: Bodley Head, 2021), 202.

● Built from 386 to 1130 CE, the Longmen Grottoes comprise more than 1,000 caves containing some of the finest examples of Buddhist Chinese sculpture. The site is now on UNESCO's World Heritage List.

● Susan Sontag, 'Melancholy Objects', in *On Photography* (New York, NY: New York Review of Books, 1977), 43.

● Ai, *1000 Years*, 200.

example, where Ai captures the artist and his partner at the time, Lu Qing, lifting her skirt in Tiananmen Square in front of a portrait of Mao Zedong. '…[T]he absurdity of the image', he writes, 'underscored the real tragedy of the now prevailing narrative that nothing at all had happened here. It was June 4, 1994, the fifth anniversary of the suppression of the democracy movement …'. ● This subversion is made more explicit in *Lu Qing and poster* (Plate 12), where Lu gives the finger to a government anti-firework campaign poster. Just by experimenting with his camera's focus and perspective, Ai also produced *Soldier on sentry duty, Tiananmen Square* (Plate 13), a work that questions what is more valued in Chinese society: the individual soldier or the collective power represented by the young man's surroundings, namely the Monument to the People's Heroes? In *Exchange* (Plate 14), a hundred US dollar bill is repeatedly exchanged into different currencies until there is not enough left to convert. Through this literal investigation of measures of financial value, Ai exposes its arbitrary nature, making plain that value is socially ascribed rather than being intrinsic.

Another way Ai makes is through unmaking. Plates 15, 16 and 17 depict him subjecting various historical objects – such as bowls and urns – to his 'little acts of mischief'. Ai's smashing or obscuring of these relics might shock the viewer into dismantling their own assumptions about worth, and what we might stand to lose or gain in the process. Creation is never far away from destruction in Ai's work. In this sense, he is a product of the ideological culture of 1960s China: 'When we were growing up, General Mao used to tell us that we can only build a new world if we destroy the old one.' ●

Finally, the series of images titled *Carpenters at work, Ai Weiwei's studio in Longzhuashu, Beijing* (Plates 19 to 22) demonstrates how the physical skill of making by hand became

important to Ai in this period of his life. Through the close study of vast volumes of antiques, he developed a strong understanding of, and appreciation for, traditional Chinese craftsmanship. 'I was deeply impressed,' he says, 'by how people thought and made objects in the past five thousand years…'. ● In these photographs, Ai documents the production of objects at the carpentry studio he set up in 1997. He collected reclaimed timber, and commissioned woodworkers and joiners to realise his experiments in furniture. Crucially for Ai, these experiments maintain the patina of the materials used, respecting their inherent 'logic' and adhering to the construction techniques of the past. This appears to be proudly announced via the close-up shots of dovetail, mortise and tenon joints, and a notable absence of screws or any other metal. The series could also be viewed as Ai realising a wish to insert himself into the lineage of makers that he so venerates. Though he is not physically engaged in the creation of these works, his patronage nevertheless enables the survival of skills that are at risk of becoming obsolete.

○

Beijing Photographs offers an important window into one decade of Ai's life. This specific period, marked by a deep exploration of China's material history and craftsmanship, left a lasting impression on Ai and his future practice. Interrogating notions of meaning – as well as the complexity of value systems and our own complicity in forming and perpetuating them – remains a preoccupation for him, and one that the artist articulates powerfully through his ongoing engagement with design. This photographic series helps us better understand how personal and historic experiences are transformed into perspectives, and how, in turn, those perspectives are made material through the works displayed in this exhibition. ○

○ Ibid., 204.
● Mathieu Wellner, 'A Talk with Ai Weiwei', in Ai Weiwei and Anthony Pins (eds), *Ai Weiwei: Spatial Matters – Art, Architecture and Activism* (London: Tate Publishing, 2014), 420.

● Interview with Karen Smith, 2005, published as part of 'Ai Weiwei: Freedom in Action', in Arturo Galansino, *Ai Weiwei: Libero* (Florence: Giunti Editore, 2016), 39.

COLLECTING CHINA

Julia Lovell

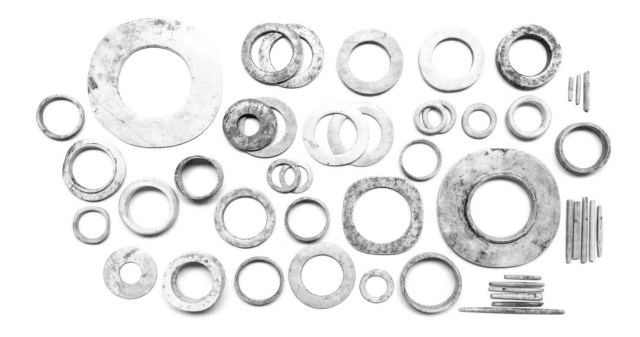

Ai Weiwei's collection of ancient jade

Ai Weiwei is internationally celebrated – and, by the Chinese government, excoriated – as a rebel. His series of photographs, *Study of Perspective* (1995–), foregrounded him giving the finger to, in turn, the White House, Hong Kong harbour and Tiananmen Square (including the latter's monumental portrait of Mao). In 2006, he called China's Communist rulers 'chunky and brainless gluttons'; in 2008, he publicised the official corruption that caused the deaths of disproportionately vast numbers of children when their schools collapsed during that year's Sichuan earthquake. Three years later, he was held in secret detention by the Chinese security service and interrogated for eighty-one days about his alleged attempts at 'state subversion'. ●

For thirty years, however, this self-identifying 'born contrarian' has practised a deeply conventional, millennia-old Chinese pastime: collecting antiquities. On returning to Beijing in 1993 from twelve years in the United States, he discovered the curios market resurgent following decades of Communist attempts to extirpate the 'old society'. Some twenty years after Mao's death in 1976, two forces combined to enable this comeback. First, frenzied construction – and foundation-digging – in China's towns and cities uncovered long-buried artefacts: every get-things-done developer had a rescue archaeologist on speed-dial. Second, business ruled: everything – from law to libidos, from cooking oil to curios – had a price. Ai and his younger brother, the novelist Ai Dan, took to haunting the antiques markets that mushroomed through the decade. 'You could find Stone Age tools, Shang and Zhou ritual vessels, jade objects from the Warring States and the Han,' Ai Weiwei recalled. 'Very soon our courtyard filled up with a huge variety of jars and vases.' ●

● For an excellent introduction to Ai Weiwei's art and activism, see Evan Osnos, 'It's Not Beautiful: An Artist Takes on the System', *New Yorker*, 24 May 2010, www.newyorker.com/magazine/2010/05/24/its-not-beautiful (accessed on 12 October 2022).

● Ai Weiwei, *1000 Years of Joys and Sorrows: A Memoir*, trans. Allen H. Barr (London: Bodley Head, 2021), 198.

From the start, Ai's collecting habits were quirky. Back in the 1990s, he recalled, 'Dealers found me perplexing, for I followed no prevailing tastes or conventional wisdom. Instead I was taken with obscure objects, and made a point of buying things that seemed to have little or no value.' ● Since then, he has accumulated thousands of Neolithic axe-heads, broken medieval teapot spouts and small, ceramic balls (originally manufactured about a millennium ago for an undetermined purpose – perhaps artillery practice). 'I think I'm the only one buying these objects,' he speculated. 'Others have more refined buying tastes: jade, porcelain. My stone axes are too early, they're not interesting enough; most people want something prettier, something more conventionally expensive-looking.' ● Never reluctant to mix media and register, Ai also hoards buttons and pieces of Lego. He has retained ceramic sherds scavenged from the ruins of his studio, which was demolished, without advance warning, by the Beijing authorities in 2018 – melancholy relics of the centre of operations from which he directed his defiant art projects for more than a decade.

Why does he collect, and in such quantities? Back in the 1990s, collecting his country's past gave Ai a distraction, a sense of security at a profoundly unsettled time. He had just returned to China after twelve eye-opening but often aimless years in the United States. His octogenarian father's health was in terminal decline. The country was emerging, uncertainly, from the political and economic ice age that had followed the government's bloody suppression of the 1989 pro-democracy movement. Beijing had changed, and was changing, dramatically – it was bigger, faster, noisier than he remembered: 'I was like a strand of duckweed floating on the water, no bonds tying it to any one place.' ● In search of anchorage, Ai struck up a new, material relationship with China's deep histories of art and craft. Day after day, he would spend hours at a time holding and studying objects made by artisans on some corner of Chinese soil hundreds and thousands of years ago, trying to connect with the skills and labour that had forged such artefacts.

> I acquired a 4,000-year-old jade axe: it had been split halfway into two very thin blades, and I couldn't figure out how it had been so perfectly shaped … I was also intrigued by an ivory talisman dating from the Shang dynasty (c.1600–1046 BCE) … the work involved in crafting this piece was so demanding, it must have taken up much of the maker's working life. Every day I would spend hours with these curios, so enamoured that my mother became jealous. ●

Ai's passion for the past has always had loud contemporary, political resonances. China in the 1990s, he judged, was still culturally malnourished after the strictures of the Mao era (1949–76). But 'art had not abandoned us – its roots were deeply planted in the weathered soil. The stubborn survival of this indigenous artistic tradition demonstrated that our narrow-minded authoritarian state would never be able to remake our culture in its own image. These things pre-dated the current order, and they would outlast it.' ● For Ai, collecting has been

Ceremonial object, Xuanji, Shang Dynasty, 1600–1046 BCE

○ Ibid., 199.
● Author's interview with Ai Weiwei, Cambridge, UK, 28 June 2022.

○ Ai, *1000 Years*, 197.
○ Ibid., 198.
● Ibid., 199.

Ai Weiwei's Left Right studio under forced demolition, 2018

a way of reconstructing – of building personal bridges with – a material history battered by decades of Communist Party rule. 'I collect,' he explained in 2022, 'for knowledge and understanding, to establish connections with my culture.' ● Ai's Song-dynasty teapot spouts are eloquent reminders of the precocious richness and abundance of Chinese arts and crafts. A thousand years ago, only the luckiest residents of the British Isles might get to possess heavy-set jugs with crudely vibrant glazes. At the same stage in China, by contrast, potters were not only able to manufacture in industrial quantities delicately refined porcelain teapots, they could also afford to reject, again in industrial quantities, components (such as Ai's sea of teapot spouts) that did not satisfy their exacting quality-control requirements. Ai's hoard of early medieval, handcrafted porcelain marbles speaks again to the abundance and high quality of materials

and labour lavished even on banal, anonymous objects such as cannonballs.

Under Mao, collecting in China was risky. History and culture could be invoked only in ways that promoted the Communist regime's ideology: 'The past,' as Mao was fond of saying, 'serves the present.' In the 1960s – peak puritanical Maoism – to collect (or in any way show respect for) the past was a potentially fatal hobby: it was evidence that you were a class enemy who worshipped the 'old society' rather than the glorious Communist present and future. When the Shanghai cosmopolitan Nien Cheng tried to persuade rampaging Red Guards not to smash her irreplaceable seventeenth-century porcelain in the opening weeks of the Cultural Revolution, they kicked her in the chest: 'You shut up! … They are the useless toys of the feudal Emperors … Our Great Leader Chairman Mao taught us, "If we do not destroy, we cannot establish."' ●

●   Author's interview.

●   Nien Cheng, *Life and Death in Shanghai* (London: Flamingo, 1995), 67.

Bubble, 2008

Ai's family, exiled in 1959 to the freezing deserts of Xinjiang due to the 'rightist' politics of Ai's famous poet father Ai Qing, also suffered in Cultural Revolution raids. Their house was thoroughly looted – books, letters, photographs and curios were confiscated and destroyed. 'The loss of these few tangible traces of my father's most personal memories,' Ai Weiwei later recalled, 'would forever impoverish my imaginings of family and society.' ● Ai's collecting impulse can be seen as a direct reaction against these experiences: 'I grew up during the Cultural Revolution, when everything old was broken or given to the government. Individuals weren't meant to collect. No one had personal belongings or private feelings associated with them.' ● Even today, when China has the second largest number of dollar billionaires in the world, after the United States, Ai denies any 'secure sense of private property' in his country. 'You could be as rich as a state, and still be taken away after

dinner and disappear.' ● One of Ai's hoards – fragments of a vast, cobalt-blue, shiny ceramic carbuncle fired in his studio ('I'd made this perfect blue bubble myself'), then destroyed in the government demolition order – embodies the precariousness of individual rights in the face of a powerful, controlling state. ●

The Cultural Revolution officially ended almost fifty years ago, but, in Ai's view, the Communist Party's project to desecrate Chinese culture survives. 'Communists are bent on destroying the old world, it's in their manifesto…They completely ruined Chinese culture.' Government-sponsored museum exhibitions, Ai argues, are 'shabby, ignorant, negligent'. Determined to vaunt the historical inevitability, and virtue, of the Communist Party, they ruthlessly ignore or excise any scholarly information that might complicate that view. 'When Communists talk about culture, they know nothing about culture. They exist against

● Ai, *1000 Years*, 133.
● Author's interview.

● Ibid.
● Ibid.

Left Right Studio Material, 2018

culture.' Disgusted by Communist stewardship of China's past, Ai seems to support — on balance — the retention by Western museums of objects removed from China during military expeditions of the nineteenth and twentieth centuries:

> The Chinese ruined their own things, by themselves. So if those things looted by Westerners hadn't been removed, they'd have been destroyed by the Chinese. Now, when they demolish Tibetan temples, truckloads of beautiful bronze Tibetan Buddhist statues are taken to factories to be melted down. So which side are you on? I think anything collected by the West is protected … collectors put them in museums, they're never going to be destroyed unless a war happens. ●

By collecting, then, Ai is contesting the right of the state to own, and speak for, China's past,

and asserting the right of the individual to build a material archive to challenge the government narrative. 'When someone buries history, it's more than I can bear. It doesn't matter if it's the history of today, or of thousands of years ago.' ●

The contrarian Ai, however, is not always a worshipful steward of China's ancient material culture, and of the labour that it cost to create it. In 1995, eager to impress his younger brother with new-fangled gadgets (in this case, the continuous-capture function on a camera), 'I had him record the last moments of a Han dynasty earthenware urn as it fell from my hands.' Despite calling the incident 'capricious, inane', Ai also justified it as 'art … as solid and authentic as that litter of earthenware shards' — the resulting photos were displayed as a triptych in 2005, and recreated in plastic bricks by Ai for an exhibition ten years later. Since 1993, Ai has regularly defaced his

● This, and references from earlier in the paragraph, are all from the author's interview.

● Ibid.

artefacts in other ways too: one of his longest-running artistic jokes has been painting the Coca-Cola logo on to intact Han dynasty urns – arguably a commentary on the brash, superficial Westernisation of China's ancient culture in the present day. The rebranding, Ai observed, in a turn of phrase reminiscent of the mercurial King Julien from the children's animation *Madagascar*, gave the original 'a lot more pizzazz'. ●

○

Ai sees little or no connection between his collecting agenda and that of previous generations. But collecting in China has been political for thousands of years. Since the beginnings of written history in Chinese, the study and ownership of ancient objects has had a profoundly moral, quasi-devotional purpose. One of China's defining thinkers, Confucius, venerated the past – its texts, objects, rituals – as a map to the natural cosmological order of things: restore the material and moral order of the sage rulers of the past, he believed, and the world will prosper. The accumulator and connoisseur of antique objects could claim to inherit the political perfection of the ancients. China's earliest dynasties, the Shang, Zhou and Qin (c.1600 BCE–200 BCE), fetishised as symbols of authority and virtue a set of nine tripod cauldrons supposedly cast by legendary sage kings of the third millennium BCE. Discussing and sharing your artefacts with like-minded individuals was fundamental to presenting yourself as a righteous man, deserving of power and influence. Although Ai claims not to 'give a damn shit' if anyone else views or appreciates his collection, there is something fervent, almost reverential about his accumulation of stuff. ● He admits to studying his antiquities obsessively, to 'finding an ethical order and a sense of beauty embedded in each piece' he encounters. ● It was a big effort – 'unthinkable, unrepeatable' – to

acquire so many objects. The peripatetic Ai moves his collection around with him, keeps it close: 'in my suitcase, under my pillow', he jokes. ●

Collecting boomed in the final 300 years of imperial rule – during the Qing dynasty, from the seventeenth to the early twentieth centuries. In Chinese versions of the European Grand Tour, scholars scoured cliffs, walls, fields, mountains and kitchens across the empire in search of traces of the past. Inscribed bronze vessels and stone steles were the most coveted pieces, but bricks, tiles and jades were also desirable. Many had a passion for ancient artefacts that bordered on addiction, declaring that they loved antiquities 'like sex' or 'a devil'. ● The modernising agronomist Luo Zhenyu – one of the greatest collectors of the early twentieth century – hoarded so many tomb figurines (buried with the deceased to stand in for the family and servants whose company they would want in the afterlife)

Luo Zhenyu (1866–1940), agronomist and collector

● Ai, *1000 Years*, 199.
● Author's interview.
● Ai, *1000 Years*, 198.

● Both quotations from author's interview.
● Shana Brown, *Pastimes: from Art and Antiquarianism to Modern Chinese Historiography* (Honolulu: University of Hawai'i Press, 2011), 53.

Ren Xun, Hu Qinhan, *Antiques from the Ke Studio*, Qing dynasty, 1644—1911 CE. Painting of antiquarian and collector Wu Dacheng

that friends nicknamed his study 'the studio of the dead'. ●

In some ways, this antiquarian pursuit seems very different from Ai's oppositional collecting impulse: it suggests a retrograde yearning by *yimin* or *yilao* — literally 'leftover people' — to escape a chaotic present and uncertain future by burying themselves in the past. Many of the most earnest late Qing collectors had lost relatives, friends and homes in the intensely destructive civil conflicts of the mid-nineteenth century. The majority collected in their spare time. In their day jobs, as officials and administrators in the imperial civil service, they grappled with the agonising economic, military and political crisis that was besetting the Chinese empire. Searching for the idealised harmony of antiquity through its objects offered such men a sense of comfort. By the end of the nineteenth century, this kind of cultural conservatism was becoming the target of ridicule. In 1894, the celebrated antiquarian Wu Dacheng was also one of the empire's senior provincial bureaucrats. When war broke out that year between the Qing and Japan, Wu volunteered to defend the Liaodong Peninsula, a slice of northeast China. His army was destroyed in one of the most ferocious collisions of the conflict. Not long after, Japan declared victory; the defeat profoundly shocked China's literate classes. Wu's critics gleefully jibed that he had been too obsessed with an ancient seal — a miniature stamp inscribed with text — proclaiming China's dominion over northeast Asia 2,000 years

earlier to size up a recently modernised, Westernised Japanese army. 'He catalogues antique jades and publishes drawings of bronze vessels … [Now he] takes out his seal and strokes it over and over. "Oh! My seal! My seal! What can I do now?"'●

Ai disassociates himself from this breed of antiquarian: 'I'm nothing like that type of collector, with their feelings of nostalgia.' ● But it would be simplistic to dismiss them all as old fogies. As officials, many sought a way for China to modernise, to compete with the vigorous, expansionist empires of the West and Japan. And in its late imperial heyday, collecting could serve radical agendas in the present, as well as a hankering for times past.

Chinese culture and politics under the Qing were dominated — as they had been for the preceding thousand years — by a handful of texts attributed to Confucius (c.500 BCE), which rulers and their civil servants were meant to pore over for insights into government. In practice, Chinese intellectuals had long challenged the authenticity, and therefore political sanctity, of these texts, which had been passed down over the millennia through different editions and oral transcriptions. This scepticism escalated after the mid-seventeenth century, when a foreign regime — the Manchu Qing, from what is now northeast China — ousted the Chinese Ming dynasty. After the Manchu conquest, China's political elite divided, very broadly, into two camps. One group accepted the new Qing government's promotion of a version of Confucianism that emphasised, through studying transmitted canonical texts,

● Chia-Ling Yang and Roderick Whitfield, 'Chronology of Luo Zhenyu (1866–1940)', in *Lost Generation: Luo Zhenyu, Qing Loyalists and the Formation of Modern Chinese Culture*, ed. Yang and Whitfield (London: Saffron, 2012), 251.

● Brown, *Pastimes*, 75.
○ Author's interview.

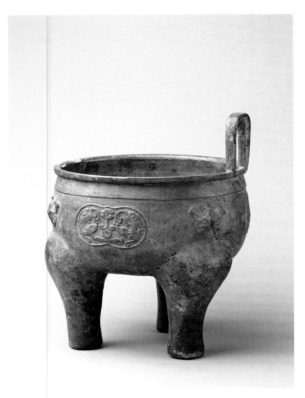

Censer, Qing dynasty, 19th to early 20th century

to – antiquity, rather than accepting dubiously transmitted texts, was key to verifying the past. An accurate understanding of history was in turn intensely relevant to present-day politics: it was fundamental to the late imperial quest to understand the sources of China's weaknesses in the face of more powerful Western and Japanese empires. In search of a rigorously evidenced history independent of published texts, antiquarians for the first time prized not just inscribed but also uninscribed artefacts (the latter type is also favoured by Ai). Out of these new practices sprang modern, scientific Chinese archaeology, capable – in theory at least – of compiling an objective account of China's past, independent of politically self-interested distortions.

The ranks of late Qing antiquarians contained some of the more radical modernisers of the day: Sun Yirang, Zhang Zhidong, Kang Youwei. Lu Xun – the 'father of modern Chinese literature', celebrated for his darkly satirical portraits of early twentieth-century China – was obsessed with ancient rubbings. Reformers often embraced antiquarianism to validate agendas for change. Some joined local assemblies – the building blocks of a parliamentary democracy – and supported progressive policies such as women's education. ● Wu Dacheng contributed to this regenerative project. His research on ancient inscriptions led him to reread early texts as undercutting the principle of absolute monarchy; in the context of the late Qing, this was deploying antiquity to question the sanctity of the emperor. ● Reformers and revolutionaries would build on such critiques of emperorship to push for constitutional monarchy and even democracy.

Although antiquarians often worked for the state, as officials, their collecting was a private, personal matter between themselves and trusted friends. Antique collections were often called 'secret hoards'; there was no concept of the public, state-sponsored museum.● Late Qing antiquarians often bemoaned the lack of libraries, museums

the political virtues of loyalty, order, duty and obedience. Another, dominated by men who refused to serve the Qing, focused their energies on so-called *kaozheng* (evidential) learning, which sought original, first-hand evidence for the teachings passed down through the ages as Confucian scripture. Disciples of this second approach valued material objects from China's deep past far more than contemporary editions of supposedly ancient texts (which – in the process of being edited, written from memory and commented on over many centuries – had absorbed multiple errors and forgeries, often introduced by manipulative rulers and their advisors). They especially prized objects that bore inscriptions – bronze vessels, stone steles – contemporary with, and therefore an authentic guide to, antiquity. ●

Between the seventeenth and nineteenth centuries, then, collecting in China became a way of questioning state orthodoxy. Studying the objects of – and contemporary witnesses

● See, for example, Benjamin A. Elman, *From Philosophy to Philology: Intellectual and Social Aspects of Change in Late Imperial China* (Leiden: Brill, 1984) and Brown, *Pastimes*.

● See, for example, Brown, *Pastimes*, 93.
● Ibid., 79.
● Ibid., 56.

Rubbing of the inscription of the Western Zhou Bronze: San Shi Pun, 1912. This rubbing has colophons by Wu Yun (1811–83) and Wu Dacheng (1835–1902)

and art galleries in China — able to classify, codify and celebrate a national past for its citizens — as 'a disgrace and a humiliation'. ● But such men — like Ai — did not rely on or trust their own state to fulfil this function. Luo Zhenyu relocated to Japan after the 1911 revolution that ended imperial rule and ushered in decades of political instability. There, he built a private library to contain and catalogue his wealth of documents and artefacts. ●

In their discordant juxtaposition of periods, media and forms — from handcrafted flints to mass-produced Lego, from medieval domestic discards to the ruins of his studio's attempt to resist the Chinese state — Ai's collections may seem mould-breaking. But they link in surprising ways to the past. The objects themselves are a physical bridge over time: between craftspeople and manufacturers of different millennia. And Ai's philosophy and practice as a collector bear the imprint of habits much older than the twentieth century. For centuries, Chinese antiquarians have appointed themselves both custodians of a revered cultural past and challengers of the status quo. Ai Weiwei inherits and celebrates this split identity. ○

● Ibid., 109.
● See Yang and Whitfield, *Lost Generation*, for more biographical information about Luo.

TO MEET BY CHANCE

Wang Shu

Ai Weiwei's first studio in Beijing, exterior, 1999

I've heard that Ai Weiwei is going to have an exhibition in London, and that he will exhibit his collection of 3,000 stone axes from the Chinese Neolithic era. This instantly evoked a memory, like Proust's little madeleine snack.

It was in 2002 that I first visited Weiwei's studio in Beijing. I invited him to teach a design studio for the new Department of Architecture that I had initiated in Hangzhou. The participants were my first architecture students, and I was the only teacher at that time. Weiwei was the first guest professor I invited.

I wanted to bring a completely different approach to this new architecture programme, a contrast to all the other boring architecture programmes taught in China. This is why I invited Weiwei.

He is the ideal teacher, to my mind, to teach not only art but also architecture. And what he taught would somehow be decisively different from what is common in Chinese universities, even though I was not sure what that difference would be.

It was already dark when I arrived at Weiwei's studio that day. He said that he designed the house himself and supervised its construction.

It was too dark to see it clearly. But I was extremely impressed – actually shocked – by the 3,000 Neolithic stone axes displayed in the indoor exhibition hall, especially when I realised that they belonged to Weiwei's collection.

I later recalled that this shock was due to at least three things: (1) the sheer materiality of the pieces and their historical nature, (2) the quantity, and (3) the fact that a contemporary artist like Weiwei was so focused on history.

What shocked me again was how relaxed Ai was in describing the stone axes, using the language of a true archaeologist.

That night, my partner Lu Wenyu and I stayed in Weiwei's studio.

The next morning, I surveyed his studio building, the professional habit of an architect.

He had paid attention to every detail.

Frankly speaking, I hadn't expected an artist to be able to make such a logically arranged house.

And the kind of spiritual atmosphere that this house invisibly expressed was not to be found elsewhere in contemporary Chinese architecture.

When I walked through the gate of the courtyard, I noticed no windows in the whole house

Ai Weiwei's first studio in Beijing, interior, 1999

except for a large floor-to-ceiling window in the living room, facing a tree in the courtyard. And this lone exterior window had been divided into small squares with white wooden mullions. (I did later find a window opening on to the narrow inner courtyard in the deepest part of the house.)

I said to Weiwei, 'Don't you like windows?'

Weiwei replied, 'No, because I'm not interested in the outside world at all! Besides, I hate glass on windows; I hate using glass on building facades; I hate that uncomfortable sparkling light of glass.'

I like Weiwei's answer. I like it for three reasons: (1) the language of architecture can express the designer's attitude towards the world, (2) this expression is direct, and (3) this expression comes from the designer's inner self-awareness.

This sort of self-awareness is generally missing among young Chinese architects. From that point of view, it can be said that Weiwei is the best architect in China.

Some people disagree with me on the grounds that Weiwei designs and builds small studios whose function is simple, but I believe that whether a building is good or bad has nothing to do with its size, but only with its attitude towards the world and its awareness of the language of architecture.

Once, Weiwei and I passed the work of a famous Chinese architect, and he said disdainfully, 'Behind the glass curtain wall is a concrete beam – how can we call it a design with so little thought?'

This is what I understand as the self-awareness of an architect.

Of course, I was shocked by his conscientiousness when I first saw Weiwei's studio in 2002. I used Chinese grey bricks in my work and so did he. We both felt strongly about the pure materiality of such bricks, but he used grey bricks for the skin and red bricks for the inside, and the transformation was simply through the bricklaying method. I wonder how Weiwei, being an artist, could understand so deeply the logic and construction language of architecture. Only a truly outstanding architect has this ability.

Model of Ai Weiwei's Beijing studio, 1999

Wang Shu and Ai Weiwei with students, 2002

I had decided to invite Weiwei to be the first visiting professor of my architecture programme before I had seen his work, not only because of the *TU MU: Young Architecture of China* exhibition we participated in together at the Aedes Gallery in Berlin in 2001, but also because of a particular detail in his exhibited work: in a model of his Beijing studio, made entirely of thin steel plates, the corners of the plates were neither welded nor folded, but were constructed like the hinges of a door. I was deeply impressed, because the attention to and refinement of the intersection of components was precisely the central feature of architectural construction.

It was said that Weiwei was the best architect among Chinese artists, but I insisted that he was the best architect in China, full stop. Some people may feel sorry for him and say it is a pity that he does not continue to practise architecture, but I don't think there is any need to feel sorry for him because he has already demonstrated what he can do.

Anyway, it turned out that I had chosen the right teacher. In late 2002, I worked with Weiwei to provide the students' first architecture studio. He and I agreed that this first studio should focus on construction, because we both agreed that constructing was a human instinct and that these students would know at least something about building houses. Weiwei proposed that the students should not be allowed to use any conventional building materials. I totally agreed with him, because

it would certainly help them to awaken their self-awareness in relation to building.

It turned out that we were not sufficiently experienced as teachers. The students were asked to build a small, three-metre by three-metre house in a corner of the college playground. After several rounds of group voting, two proposals were chosen: one using recycled plastic cola bottles and the other using discarded bicycles found all over the college. Even though the students worked on the houses continuously – working every day just like a real construction team, as requested by Weiwei – they could not finish the houses in time for the end of the term. So the bottle group, under my guidance, worked in the snow to complete their construction over the winter break. The bicycle group, on the other hand, went to Weiwei's studio in Beijing to spend Chinese New Year together there, and completed their assignment with the help of craftspeople from Weiwei's studio.

Despite the students having had to work during the holidays, I think this construction studio conveyed to them a spirit that they will remember for the rest of their lives.

I still have a special interest in Weiwei's approach to history. I remember one of his widely known works involved shattering antique Chinese jars at a museum exhibition. Many people were stunned by this, but, from my perspective, the demolition of almost all traditional Chinese cities in the last few decades was a much larger scale of destruction than the breaking of these jars. What had shocked me was rather that people were almost indifferent to the destruction of

Detail of Xiangshan Campus, Academy of Art, Hangzhou, China, 2016

Detail of a wall at the Ningbo History Museum, Zhejiang, 2017

their own traditions on such a scale. What's more, the sheer scale of this destruction, in terms of materials, astonished me.

I think what often impresses people when they visit Weiwei's exhibitions is the materiality of civilisations, and the impact of this materiality on the human mind is only magnified by its quantity and scale.

When I started to design the Xiangshan Campus of the China Academy of Art in Hangzhou in 2002, the reason why I chose to use seven million recycled bricks and tiles was precisely because of this huge blank gulf between history and reality, which is where my thinking intersected with Weiwei's. I felt that a contemporary architect must respond to the wholesale demolition of traditional buildings in China. This is not only a question of thinking about recycling from an ecological perspective, but also a question of how to maintain the dignity of the culture to which one belongs.

From what I know about Weiwei, his dedication to traditional Chinese culture goes far beyond what one might expect.

One year, around 2004, he bought a Ming dynasty chair in Hangzhou. When he returned to Beijing, he thought it would be inconvenient to bring it with him, so he said to me, 'Let's put it in your studio first.'

The special thing about this chair was that it was at the time the only chair that could be definitively identified as being from the Ming dynasty (206 BCE–220 CE), because it had a chronology on the back handwritten by a Ming dynasty official.

Weiwei is very forthright. This chair was in my possession for four or five years. Suddenly, one day, he said he wanted someone to come and collect it. I was a little reluctant, so I asked a graduate student to help me move the chair downstairs on to the pavement of the city street; then I sat on it, watching people and vehicles come and go. I did not know the fate of this chair.

Later, I read in an article that Weiwei had used the chair as a model and made many copies of it in marble.

When the chair was placed in my studio, I was working on the design and construction of the Ningbo History Museum. Faced with thirty traditional villages that had been demolished by the city government to make way for a new business district nicknamed 'Little Manhattan', I insisted on collecting one million old bricks and tiles from the villages, which were mixed with a fair-faced concrete textured with bamboo formwork to build the interior and exterior skins of the building.

In the contrast between these materials, a new meaning is conveyed. We need to keep some memories and hope.

I often feel, as Borges has written, that Ai Weiwei and I are walking in a garden with forking paths.

Or, perhaps, walking in *The Waste Land* with forking paths. ○

Ai Weiwei, *Marble chair*, 2008

I FELT THE WIND, THE AIR...

Brian Dillon

Dropping a Han Dynasty Urn, 1995

One of the half-cities is permanent, the other is temporary,
and when the period of its sojourn is over, they uproot it,
dismantle it and take it off, transplanting it to the vacant
lot of another half-city.

Italo Calvino,
Invisible Cities (1972)

The most amazing thing is that history is being
antiquated as vague terrain.

Jean Baudrillard,
'The Anorexic Ruins' (1989)

There are ruins everywhere in Ai Weiwei's art.
This is in some ways an obvious thing to say, at
least if one takes 'ruin' to mean simply the act of
(partial) destruction and its material aftermath.
An inaugural moment for this tendency: a
triptych of photographs of the artist *Dropping
a Han Dynasty Urn* (1995). Like three frames of
a cartoon, or stills from an especially stark and
simple bit of slapstick. (No irony, no punchline,
no reprieve: this apparent act of vandalism is
genuine after all.) The 2,000-year-old artefact
is at first precariously held, then unbelievably
airborne, and finally lies in fragments at the
artist's feet, while his hands are still comedically
splayed in the moment of letting go. In an
interview twenty years later, Ai said: 'I wouldn't
call it being destroyed — it just has another life.' ●

Ai's defence of this work — or rather the
gesture the work depicts — is a neat way of saying

that the moment of ruination is both the
beginning and the end of a process. Ruins
always project us forward into an unknowable
future, quite as much as they ask us to reflect
on, or mourn, a vanishing past. In Ai's work,
this temporal hinge — the instant of breaking
and remaking — is sometimes clearly signalled:
we can literally see the fractures and the joins,
the places where history has been smashed and
repaired, wounded and (this may not be the
right word) healed. This mended rupture is
most obvious in the works that remodel old and
sometimes properly ancient objects: a temple,
a tree, a house, antique wooden furniture
carved up and reconstituted, its limbs at odd
new angles, articulating — what?

Just as it is never, emotionally or aesthetically,
only nostalgic or melancholic, the ruin is rarely
a politically neutral entity. Ruins may result from

● Ai Weiwei, in Tim Marlow, 'Ai Weiwei in Conversation', *Ai Weiwei*
(London: Royal Academy of Arts, 2015), 20.

or represent decay, of course; but abandonment can also be a violent act. Frequently, the ruin of a building, a city or a landscape reminds us of a sudden or protracted act of war, atrocity or exploitation. Even natural disasters are never purely natural. So it is with Ai's ruins, which variously recall: his childhood exile with his father (the poet Ai Qing), including time in a subterranean dwelling (there is a hint of this space in *Water Lilies #1* [2022]); the physical as well as psychological architecture of Ai's own incarceration by the state; the headlong demolition and redevelopment of Chinese cities, and consequent disappearing of historic buildings and infrastructure; the devastation wrought by the Sichuan earthquake of 2008, and official efforts to hide the reasons for the scale of destruction and death caused — and to conceal even the names of schoolchildren who died. This is an art of ruin that, in keeping with the most ancient and venerated ruins, has one eye on what might be made of all this in the future.

○

Robert Smithson, *The Monuments of Passaic*, Passaic, NJ, USA, 1967

In the October 1967 issue of *Artforum* magazine, the land artist Robert Smithson published an essay (with accompanying photographs) titled 'A Tour of the Monuments of Passaic, New Jersey'. Though he didn't mention the fact, Smithson was returning to the town where he was born. On the post-industrial outskirts of Passaic, a new highway was being built: 'River Drive was in part bulldozed and in part intact. It was hard to tell

the new highway from the old road; they were both confounded in a unitary chaos.' ● Along the river, Smithson discovers what he insists are 'monuments': a row of pipes protruding from the bank, a mid-stream derrick and an abandoned children's sandpit as he nears the centre of town. Passaic, the artist concludes ironically, is the modern American successor to Rome's eternal city. A place disappearing and coming into being at the same time. A city of ruins — but 'ruins in reverse'. ●

Vacated barracks, a dismantled power plant, numerous low-rise dwellings in varied conditions of near-erasure: Ai's photographic series *Provisional Landscapes* (2002–8) shows a busy texture of urban and exurban life being obliterated. The photographs are unpopulated, and they are generally composed of three strata: a foreground of sparse debris or nothing much (a no-man's land, a *terrain vague*); in the middle distance, some abandoned or half-demolished structures of an older style; and, beyond these, sometimes hazy and sometimes toweringly vivid, the new construction rising without conscience above the wreckage. Building and demolition in the same image and the same instant — but this is not quite what Smithson intends by 'ruins in reverse'. He means it is all disappearing and coming to be at the same time: the antique past being churned up and flung into new life (like the shattered urn), the brand-new offices and apartment blocks already derelict ghosts of the future they promise.

When we deploy the aesthetic category of the ruin, we usually mean by it a simple building fallen into desuetude, a process that begins 'naturally' with abandonment or has been triggered by a single violent, perhaps deliberate, act. (Are new or fresh ruins really 'ruins'? In her classic study *Pleasure of Ruins*, the scholar and novelist Rose Macaulay — who had lost her London home in the Blitz — remarks that eventually such ruins will be softened and romanticised by nature and time but, for a

● Robert Smithson, *The Collected Writings*, ed. Jack Flam (Berkeley, CA: University of California Press, 1996), 71.
● Ibid., 72.

Provisional Landscapes, 2002–8

Template, 2007. Photo taken after its collapse

while, 'blackened and torn, they smell of fire and mortality'. ●) But the ruin is never simply one thing, one structure, any more than it belongs only to one moment in time. Ruination leaks out, invades and flourishes — it cannot be contained. In Ai's work, the ruin seems to ramify, to become a field of forms or a swarm of matter, something endlessly articulable into new shapes, arrangements and structures. You can see this in a work such as *Template* (2007), made of wooden doors and windows from Ming and Qing dynasty houses, but also in a more directly personal and political work like *Left Right Studio Material* (2018): thousands of fragments of porcelain from Ai's sculptures, destroyed when the Chinese government demolished his studio.

In the history of ruins and art in European culture, the Lisbon earthquake of 1755 plays a pivotal role. For most of the century, this singular catastrophe stands in the artistic, literary and philosophical imagination for the blank, unsparing fact of disaster: something that can't be subsumed or rehabilitated into metaphysical or religious meaning. To study such events, writes Immanuel Kant in 'On the Causes of Earthquakes' (1756), means rejecting superstitious explanations in favour of cold evidence and scientific inquiry:

> Great events that affect the fate of all mankind rightly arouse that commendable curiosity, which is stimulated by all that is extraordinary and typically looks into the causes of such events. In such cases, the natural philosopher's obligation to the public is to give an account of the insights yielded by observation and investigation. ●

In the case of the Sichuan earthquake, Ai adopted the role of citizen investigator, tasked with pursuing the truth on behalf of the families of the 5,197 children who perished, and whose names were being withheld by the authorities.

● Rose Macaulay, *Pleasure of Ruins* (London: Thames & Hudson, 1984), 454.

● Immanuel Kant, *Natural Science*, ed. Eric Watkins (Cambridge: Cambridge University Press, 2012), 327.

Some of the black-and-white photographs that Ai produced of the aftermath of that earthquake have the somewhat distanced style of the *Provisional Landscapes* series: debris in the foreground, ruined buildings and, in this case, mountains preceding overall. Other images bring us closer to the unseen horror: backpacks, schoolbooks and pencil cases strewn on the ground. The more detached but thorough visual correlative for the citizen's investigation is to be found in Ai's video footage of the ruins of school buildings: here, an engineer reveals the inadequate construction materials that could not withstand the earthquake and so sealed the children's fate. In 2009, Ai published on his blog as many names as he had been able to discover, and made of the list a wall-text work simply titled *Names of the Student Earthquake Victims Found by the Citizens' Investigation* (2008–11).

Interviewed in 2015, Ai said:

> I went to the disaster area, to these ruins. Standing in the earthquake zone, I felt the wind, the air, it was really horrifying: you have bodies underneath the rubble and you feel the wind, you feel that death is there. ●

Chinese rescue workers put together the schoolbags found in the ruins of a building of Hongbai Town Central Elementary School, which collapsed because of an earthquake in Hongbai Town, Shifang city, Sichuan province, China, on 15 May 2008

○

The most resonant work emerging from the earthquake is *Straight* (2008–12). Ai began buying up tonnes of twisted reinforcement bars from destroyed or damaged buildings, and employed a team of workers to straighten them out again: an arduous process of hammering by hand. In all, 200 tonnes of metal were repaired or repurposed in this fashion; during the work, Ai was incarcerated, and on his release returned to his studio to hear hammers ringing on steel: the labourers had carried on in his absence. ●
In the resulting installation, the rust-brown bars lie parallel in drifts or strata, forming a kind of map or landscape: a flattened but expansive rendering, or rather implication, of the ruined schools, and an invocation of the lost children.

Among the insights of Smithson's writing on modern ruins (it's surely already there in the ruin aesthetics of the eighteenth century) is that what we think of as landscape is already evidence of destruction and decay – whether the vast alterations of geology or the interventions and abandonments of industry and agriculture. Everywhere Smithson looks he sees a world in splinters, being recomposed. In 'The Crystal Land' (1966), he visits a New Jersey quarry and reflects:

> Fragmentation, corrosion, decomposition, disintegration, rock creep, debris slides, mud flow, avalanche were everywhere in evidence. The grey sky seemed to swallow

● Marlow, 'Conversation', 22.
● Some of these metal fragments were also used for the series *Forge* (2008–12).

Straight, 2008–12

up the heaps around us. Fractures and faults spilled forth sediment, crushed conglomerations, eroded debris and sandstone. It was an arid region, bleached and dry. An infinity of surfaces spread in every direction. A chaos of cracks surrounded us. ●

There is assuredly something of this ruined version of landscape in Ai's work. Again, *Provisional Landscapes* is the most obvious example: Beijing, in the years before the 2008 Olympics, being transformed temporarily into a desolate version of the picturesque, new and old structures supplying the equivalent of landforms and landmarks, what little vegetation remains (a patch of grass, an isolated tree) adding compositional elements that seem to parody landscape painting of

the past. The earthquake photographs too: in their monochrome austerity, in the reduction of buildings and lives to so much debris at the foot of the mountains. But there are other modes of ruinous landscape in Ai's art, and they are not quite reducible to either mourning or fury at what is passing away or already defunct. If the rescued rebar in *Straight* looks like a territory or its relief map, there's a precedent in Ai's many works that pile up or strew found materials, antique or modern. The 4,434 Neolithic stone tools in *Still Life* (1993–2000) are arranged in a flat display that compacts their history and geographic diversity to a single plane. In *Spouts* (2015), hundreds of thousands of antique teapot spouts from the Song dynasty (960–1279 CE) look at first glance like a field of bones. But something is given new life here – dead or disregarded objects start to

● Smithson, *Collected Writings*, 9.

seem like conduits, tiny mouths or trumpets to project voices as yet unheard.

A ruin given new life, opened to the future as well as the past — this seems like the very definition of another cultural and aesthetic category: the monument. (Smithson again: 'Passaic seems full of "holes" compared to New York City, which seems tightly packed and solid, and those holes in a sense are the monumental vacancies that define, without trying, the memory-traces of an abandoned set of futures.' ●) A monument hovers between times, and its purchase on time-past and time-to-come can seem precarious. Between 1995 and 2011, Ai took photographs of familiar, easily recognisable artistic and architectural icons, before all of which he raised his left middle finger: the Eiffel Tower, the *Mona Lisa*, the Colosseum, the Palace of Westminster,

Trump Tower. Transformed into pigment prints and exhibited as *Study of Perspective* (2022), these images record the comic affronting of the monument, simultaneously an acknowledgement of its status and a mischievous reduction — in the case of already antique sites like the Colosseum, we might speak here of a *ruin ruined*. But, in a sense, ruins are always ruined to another degree: their fate is to live on, beyond their first life and beyond its end, into an unpredictable future. It is this aspect that Ai takes advantage of in his work, this future into which time and again he casts us, with irony and sincerity. ○

● Ibid., 72.

ONE HUNDReD THOUSAND THINGS

Justin McGuirk

Still Life, 1993–2000

You walk into a large gallery and encounter a field of Neolithic tools laid out on the floor. There are about 4,000 of them: axe-heads, hatchets, chisels, spools and other rudimentary instruments with which our ancestors carved out an existence in the late Stone Age. Any one of these might be a museum piece, sitting in a glass case with a label that reads: 'Chisel, c.4000 BCE, stone'. But here are thousands of them, with no labels, cases or other museological garnishes. We are not used to seeing them assembled in such numbers. They have been derarefied. Stripped of their uniqueness, they are more of a terrain, a geological layer exposed to reveal *Homo faber*'s early technical abilities.

This work, *Still Life*, is one of a series of Ai Weiwei's assemblages in which he gathers objects in bewildering numbers. In the same gallery, the visitor will encounter a field of 250,000 porcelain spouts from Song dynasty teapots and wine ewers, and 200,000 porcelain cannonballs. Next to these are fields of porcelain fragments and Lego pieces that are not even counted but simply measured by weight or square metre. Numerous artists, from Arman to Warhol, have created assemblages of repeated objects, but Ai is operating on a completely different scale. He is the Cecil B. DeMille of the multiple, deploying his cast of thousands across the battlefield of the gallery.

How are we to read these fields of objects? What do they signify? Visitors who know Ai Weiwei the iconoclast – the artist who smashes Han dynasty vases and gives landmark buildings the middle finger – will encounter a figure who is, in fact, deeply invested in history. Ai's lifetime happens to have coincided with a period of Chinese history when history itself was devalued by zealous modernisers and overridden by a relentless development drive. On display here are not just things but lost histories of making. The aesthetic sensibilities and craft know-how embodied in the things themselves have been forgotten – if not in theory, then certainly wiped from muscle memory. The artefacts are therefore a form of testimony to those pasts – a vast haul of evidence, if you like.

That is the first way to read these fields and, thus far, I have Ai's blessing. But the other argument I will go on to make is that these objects point to the fact that there are alternative histories of technology to be written. One might think that a chronological arrangement of objects that starts with stone tools and ends with injection-moulded Lego bricks tells a universal story of human technical progress. In fact, China has a history of technology that exists in parallel with the dominant Western narrative, stemming from different origin myths and embodying a distinct ethical tradition. Ai's prodigious collecting of historical artefacts is, I would argue, a quest in search of an ethic that he feels has largely disappeared from modern China. One might even say that it is absent from technological discourse in general. But, before exploring those ideas, we should begin by looking more closely at the things themselves and consider what picture of civilisation they conjure.

Contemplating a field of 250,000 porcelain spouts, one could be forgiven for mistaking them for bones. It is as if a great ossuary has been exhumed and dumped on the gallery floor. On discovering that they are actually bone-china spouts, the first question that comes to mind is, 'Why just the spouts?' In Jingdezhen, the city of kilns where these were made one thousand years ago, if a pot was not perfect then the spout was broken off. And so, while we are presented with what is essentially a waste stream, these hundreds of thousands of rejects attest to the rigorous aesthetic standards of the Song dynasty. They also ought to prompt a certain cognitive

Inside the large kiln at the Jingdezhen Ceramic Museum, China

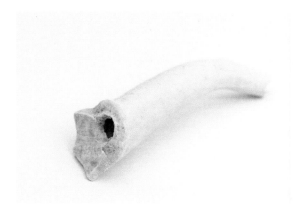

Detail of *Spouts*, 2015

dissonance in those of us who are products of British schooling: didn't industrial-scale pottery begin in Stoke-on-Trent in the late eighteenth century? Hardly, but we shall come back to that. As ever with Ai, there is a resonance in these objects with his criticisms of contemporary China, in that the broken spouts – or mouths – could symbolise free speech that has been stifled. This subtext rises closer to the surface when one recalls the stories of citizens being invited to 'take tea' at the local police station – a euphemism for an interrogation.

Adjacent to the spouts is a field of perfect spheres, some the size of marbles and others slightly smaller than golf balls. Ai himself had no idea what these were when he first encountered them. They smelled slightly of gunpowder and had been unearthed from a moat surrounding a fortress in Dingzhou. It turned out they were cannon shot made of high-quality Xing ware porcelain produced during the Northern Qi and Song dynasties (550–1279 BCE). At first, Ai was confused as to whether they were handmade or industrially manufactured but, when it became clear that no two cannonballs were identical, the scale of the handicraft required brought the dawning of a new aspect. Imagine the technique and precision required to hand-make 200,000 spheres. And what kind of civilisation wages war with porcelain weaponry?

We might ask what category of artwork we are dealing with here. We tend to think of Ai operating in the mode of his heroes Marcel

Duchamp and Andy Warhol, transposing base readymades into finely crafted sculptures of marble, or daubing them with house paint. But these tools, spouts and cannonballs are less readymades than they are found objects in the Surrealist tradition. They are elemental curios rife with different associations and interpretations. And many were picked up at flea markets, just as was André Breton's habit. On returning to Beijing in 1993, after more than a decade in the United States, Ai began frequenting the Panjiayuan flea market on the outskirts of the city. There, he encountered artefacts that sparked a deep curiosity about Chinese history, and in particular its cultures of craftsmanship. At the flea market, Ai discovered 'an ethical order and a sense of beauty embedded in each piece I encountered'. ● And the pieces were going for almost nothing. Mao's Cultural Revolution, with its injunction to smash all remnants of feudal and bourgeois culture, had prepared the ground for another wave of destruction in the 1990s and 2000s, this time driven by the property market. The message was clear: history, or at least vast swathes of it, was worthless.

Ai gained a reputation as a major collector, and not just of fine craftsmanship but also of the kind of material that other collectors would have no interest in – teapot spouts, for instance. Soon the objects were finding *him*. And his ability to attract vast quantities of things is what makes the artworks unique, because we are not dealing here with artefacts displayed as collections, but collections presented as artworks. It is their numerousness that defines them. If we return to the question of what category they belong to, we can only answer: none. Duchamp's readymade treats an industrially manufactured object as unique, whereas Ai presents 100,000 handmade things as somehow generic. Both positions trade in irony, but they are opposites. Ai's works are closer to Breton's *objet trouvé* (found object), which also tended to be a craft object rather than an industrial one, but enter a different realm because of their sheer number. I proposed to Ai

Panjiayuan market in Beijing, China, 2008

that we call them 'fields' because of their terrain-like quality, to which he agreed. And it is true that in their planar dimension they have the character of indoor land art. But I might also have called them 'gatherings'. This is not because they consist of many things gathered together, but because the very idea of the 'thing' embodies a gathering. As many philosophers, from Martin Heidegger to Bruno Latour, have pointed out, the etymology of 'thing' has its roots in Norse and Germanic words for assembly or parliament. These meetings were where matters of concern were discussed, but over time the meaning shifted to things themselves as material culture and possessions became more and more the focus of people's concern. The fields, as we shall see, have a political content that resonates with those original gatherings.

If we borrow Heidegger's highly simplistic distinction between an 'object' (factual, scientific,

● Ai Weiwei, *1000 Years of Joys and Sorrows: A Memoir*, trans. Allen H. Barr (London: Bodley Head, 2021), 198.

Detail of *Sunflower Seeds*, 2010

industrial) and a 'thing' (handmade, imbued with human poetry), it is then clear that Ai's fascination with Chinese historical artefacts lies in their *thingness*. The 'ethical order' and 'sense of beauty' he found in the artefacts in Panjiayuan spoke to a culture of craftsmanship and aesthetic care that Ai found to be missing from modern China. The country had refashioned itself as the factory of the world, the land of cheap labour, and with that shift had embraced a low-grade materialism writ large in everything from consumer goods to infinitely repeated tower blocks. In that sense, the very act of collecting these things was a form of dissent. As Ai writes, 'The stubborn survival of this indigenous artistic tradition demonstrated that our narrow-minded authoritarian state would never be able to remake our culture in its own image.' ● In a country where memory could be weakened or erased through censorship or by the revisionist state media, here was hard evidence of thousands

of years of artisanal and design culture that embodied higher aspirations.

The tension that crackles off the fields is between the craftsmanship contained in a single artefact and the industrial scale of their number. We are confronted with quantities of human skill, labour and time that feel unmeasurable. Contemplating a field of 200,000 almost identical but handmade porcelain cannonballs can summon a sense of the sublime: an inability to comprehend the display's fearsome proportions. One hesitates to celebrate it, because, aside from the skill, what drudgery it must have entailed. I felt the same about another of Ai's field works, *Sunflower Seeds*, first displayed in Tate Modern's Turbine Hall. Imagine commissioning a hundred million replica seeds hand-painted on porcelain — the care and detail coupled with the repetitive labour of thousands of pairs of hands.

This is machinic work. As a young artist, Ai identified with one of Warhol's maxims: 'I think

● Ibid., 199.

Detail of *Untitled (Porcelain Balls)*, 2022

everybody should be a machine.' It offered a sardonic form of identity and structure. I mentioned earlier that one of the fields consists of thousands of Lego pieces. Ai likes to create images in Lego precisely because, as an objective system, it depersonalises the result, removing any traces of the artist's hand or taste. The cannonballs and spouts were also the product of artisans working within systems, working to a high standard of perfection. As the Lego works suggest, Ai has no interest in developing or exercising such skill himself – he leaves that to his master artisans. But he is clearly fascinated by the contradiction of handmade objects with a machine-like output. One wonders what Walter Benjamin would have made of this art from the age of non-mechanical reproduction.

This tension, embodied in craftsmanship on an industrial scale, lies at the very root of China's unique history of technics. We tend to think of the Industrial Revolution as the cradle of mass production, yet China had mass production for thousands of years – just without the steam power. Indeed, China had factories as early as the Shang period (1650–1050 BCE). It employed standardisation, modularity and the division of labour – all of which we think of as industrial systems – in bronze casting, architecture, porcelain production and woodblock printing. The soldiers of the Terracotta Army, created around 210 BCE, were fashioned from modular legs, torsos and heads. Who made them? The same people who made drainage pipes. Yet a great deal of fine craftsmanship was involved in the facial features and the armour, for central to the magical properties of this fake army in the afterlife was its verisimilitude to a real one. ●

With modularity and mass production come obvious constraints on personal freedom, both artistically and socially. Everyone has their place in a modular system, which can

● The making of the Terracotta Army is well explained in Lothar Ledderose, *Ten Thousand Things: Module and Mass Production in Chinese Art* (Princeton, NJ: Princeton University Press, 2000). It is also worth noting that the concept of 'the ten thousand things'

comes from the *Dao De Jing* and is commonly read as a reference to the material diversity of the world.

The world-famous Terracotta Army, part of the Mausoleum of the first Qin Emperor and a UNESCO World Heritage Site located in Xian, China

Jade axe, Longshan culture, Neolithic era

inculcate the kinds of hierarchy and conformity that Ai chafes against. This is not, then, a romantic vision of craftsmanship, of the free artisan, but the factory vision. One has to remember that when Ai invokes a bygone 'ethical order' in the things at the flea market, he was also collecting much more refined artefacts — his collection of jade, for instance, is extraordinary. The fields are not about instances of fine craftsmanship but the skill that went into even the most ubiquitous things. Ai is not romanticising the assembled ranks of artefacts so much as revelling in the mystery and contradiction that they present to the contemporary mind.

And it is here that I believe the fields offer a possible departure point for problematising the contemporary understanding of technology. In their display of craftsmanship on an industrial scale, the fields emblematise a facet of China's technical history that is unique and that bears deeper consideration. They remind us that China was the supreme technical civilisation for thousands of years before the Industrial Revolution. This very fact led the British scientist and Sinologist Joseph Needham to ask why it was that modern science and technology emerged in the West rather than in China. In the traditional historical account, which has no doubt been over-simplified, China was in fact resistant to Western technology until its defeat by the British in the Opium Wars, an event the Chinese blamed on their technological shortcomings. This calamity triggered a rapid modernisation in the interests of competing with the West. Is this the juncture at which China abandoned the 'ethical order' Ai admires in favour of a Western conception of technics?

The Berlin-based Chinese philosopher Yuk Hui makes the case that China's history of technics is unique — indeed, he argues that technics never existed in China in the way we understand them today. We tend to think of technology as being a universal human output, but Hui reminds us that *techne* is a Greek word whose very meaning is rooted in the Promethean myth of the theft of fire. Those origins remain embedded in the – arguably Western – sense of agency we have as beings who dominate the world with our technical prowess. In China, by contrast, technology has different mythological origins and belongs to a whole other moral cosmology. Hui argues that, in Confucianism, the use of tools (*qi*) is connected to heaven through *dao* (harmony). In this cosmology, the tool – or what we might just call technology – is nothing without the exercise of *dao*, which is more than merely the skill to use that tool but an ethical way of exercising it. Hui turns to Zhuangzi's tale of the butcher Pao Ding by way of illustration. In butchering a cow, Pao Ding never cuts tendons or bones, but skilfully finds the path of least resistance, demonstrating that *dao* is more important than the knife. I like to pair this in my mind with a shopping-channel ad for a power blade that 'cuts right through tendons and bones!' Here the technological determinism of the tool has dispensed with *dao* in favour of dollars.

Central to Hui's argument is the principle that Confucianism never treated the tool in isolation, for its mastery was linked to a perfection of being – the unity of *qi* and *dao*. Is this the 'ethical order' that Ai read in the historical artefacts at the flea market? There is an argument that the holistic technical ethics that defined Chinese craftsmanship for thousands of years were gradually abandoned with the adoption of Western mechanisation. The Chinese, Hui argues, believed they could import Western technology without affecting their own cosmology, but mechanisation necessitated an inevitable transformation of mind. You can't make craftsmanship redundant and sustain the craftsman's worldview. And Confucianism itself was later repudiated as backward superstition during the Cultural Revolution. Hui writes: 'Modernisation is fundamentally a transformation, if not a destruction, of the moral cosmology that is expressed in every form of art in China,

from tea ceremonies to calligraphy, from craftsmanship to architecture.' ●

One could reasonably argue that industrialisation and modernity were destructive to an ethic of craftsmanship and care not just in China but around the world. There is little doubt that the modern approach to technics, as exemplified by digital technologies, has led to technological determinism, deskilling and the global homogenisation of technicity. For Hui, that only makes it all the more urgent to distinguish between diverse forms of technical thought. The question is, how does this relate to Ai's position? It is hard to think of an artist less nostalgic or romantic, and he does not preach a Confucian espousal of *dao*. He is, if anything, an early adopter who embraces social media and a Western model of individual freedom that he finds painfully absent in his own country. Yet there is no separating the 'ethical order' he finds in Chinese historical artefacts from the moral cosmology that produced them. The value he recognises lies in more than just skilled craftsmanship, but rather in an aesthetic sensibility that treats objects not just as technical outcomes, but as things that have a rounded sense of human relations impressed on them through their making.

In the fields, then, we see not only a new approach to the multiple in art but evidence on a mass scale of a unique strain of technical thought in China. Ai has spent decades discovering and reconnecting with a moral cosmology in which skill and craftsmanship are centre stage. The fact that he feels this ethical dimension has largely disappeared from contemporary China suggests that the fields expose the myth of progress – we may gain in technicity, but we also lose skills and ethical qualities along the way. And, finally, the fields testify to the power of history in the face of a state-led culture that has only a selective use for it. Ai's great project has been not just exposing lost cultural values, but unearthing a China that he can believe in. ○

● Yuk Hui, *The Question Concerning Technology in China: An Essay in Cosmotechnics* (Falmouth: Urbanomic Media Ltd, 2017), 224.

In
Conversation

Eyal Weizman and Ai Weiwei

Ai Weiwei and his selection of 4,434 stone tools for the Design Museum exhibition (from his collection of 16,134 pieces), 2023

Eyal Weizman is the founder of Forensic Architecture, a research agency that uses spatial and architectural analysis to investigate human rights violations. Weizman's work shares several themes with Ai Weiwei's, from challenging official narratives to establishing a body of work linked to violence or destruction. In this conversation, Weizman and Ai discuss their respective approaches to gathering evidence. They address shifting attitudes in archaeology, how fragments are used to piece together events and the speed at which a crack moves through an object.

AI WEIWEI
I am happy to be having this conversation. Looking at your work, I really respect the way you collect evidence and structure another image of the truth. The truth is not simply there, except when we identify it clearly. Very often we say, 'Truth is truth, it happened.' However, how is it to be analysed, or narrated? One really needs a clear method for that. My studio does a lot of research too, we have done so ever since the Sichuan earthquake, but we never really use this analytical approach, which is an architectural way of restructuring our memory. Our memory is a fragment — it is shattered. Someone has to restructure it. Who's going to do that? At first glance, you wouldn't immediately say that our show is a normal exhibition about design, but rather about historical evidence. Evidence for me is so important, because it really defines who we are in different times. For example, the early Neolithic tools I collect, or the wine and tea spouts, or my broken porcelain work, and Lego. Evidence exists as facts, and those facts are such an important element in the idea of design. Very often, we think design comes from our own taste, habits or style, but if we look at the larger historical perspective, it's something that is inevitable. It's not up to our desires, but rather up to our needs. I don't know if you feel the same way about the materials you're gathering.

EYAL WEIZMAN
I was very interested when I saw that the exhibition deals with the Neolithic period. That time is very much of interest to me, particularly the transformation between hunter-gatherers

and settler societies, the beginning of cities. I'm currently working with the archaeologist David Wengrow, who has recently written an important book called *The Dawn of Everything*, together with David Graeber. This book looks at the transition between hunter-gatherers and agriculturists. With David we have looked further at the paradigm shift happening in archaeology over the past few decades. In the imperial-era archaeology of the nineteenth century, the gathering of evidence was based on the concept of 'unearthing', meaning you take something from the ground and clean the earth from it. Earth is the noise, and the object is the signal. The earth is holding the signal. But contemporary archaeologists are actually undertaking a figure-ground inversion and are interested in the soil itself. The soil includes anthropogenic signals — evidence of fire, cultivation, pollen, magnetism, etc. In that sense, inverting the figure-ground relationship is very interesting. It's a different kind of archaeology, a gentler one, which is not based on objects but on prospecting the earth through different optics. You can then use all sorts of technologies, equivalent to ultrasound, and you can start seeing forms come up from the earth. The cities that come from the Neolithic era — 7,000 or 9,000 years ago — and in different places in the world, are not cities as we know them. The book I mentioned shows many cities that have no hierarchy, no temples, no big burial sites, no military, no fences and no walls. It makes me think, 'How can we read the history of the world differently?' I'm interested in how archaeological evidence shifts from the object to patterns between objects, or to the ground. When I saw your work *Still Life*, with thousands of stone tools laid out together, I felt that there was something in it that defetishises the object, which I think was archaeology's problem. It would take a treasure out of the earth and discard everything that was above it. In my country, in Palestine, Israel, the state is interested only in one period of archaeology: the biblical. Everything above it — for example, Islamic archaeology, Mamluk archaeology, Ottoman archaeology, contemporary Palestinian daily life — is thrown away in order to get to the biblical object. The question really is, 'How to defetishise this object?'

AW

That's interesting. When we give meaning to an object, we think it's important. We pick it up to unearth it, and this shows our ignorance about everything that has been wiped away. It is impossible to understand that part of the object. Those Stone Age tools I collect come from markets. They were not dug up, but rather gathered by farmers or shepherds, and then are sold at the markets. They think these must be important objects. They know they are not organic objects, they're handmade. They know how difficult it is to make a piece of rock like that. It's impossible for such tools to be made today. In the market, of course, there are also other objects that are more precious, like a jade axe, which is highly polished and judged highly for its aesthetics, treated as though it has a lot of meaning. By comparison, those stones are not so important. The objects these traders sell are quite cheap, which gave me the opportunity to collect them. The reason I collect them is because I know they carry a meaning beyond my understanding. You can see these objects were so important for their time, probably the only possessions people had in their lifetime, and passed on to their children. For me, it's fun to imagine how they functioned, and why they have these particular forms.

EW

I'm interested by the fact that these objects were found not by archaeologists but by farmers. They found the tools of farmers who farmed there 7,000 years before them. I imagine they have an appreciation of these tools. Only two generations ago, you would still use an ox to farm. Now they use tractors, but there is still a hard object that cuts the earth and the user can see themselves cultivating. This is a kind of continuous culture.

I love that these archaeological objects are found by non-archaeologists. And I want to make a jump from this kind of object to evidence produced by non-professionals. When I saw these tools, to me they all looked somewhat like smartphones, iPhones perhaps, as they are similar in size. The evidence that can be produced today by non-professionals is a massive transformation in our understanding of who has the ability, and

Detail of *Still Life*, 1993–2000

the right, to produce evidence, and what constitutes evidence in a legal and human rights context. For me, that stone found by a farmer is almost like in the movie *2001: A Space Odyssey* [Stanley Kubrick, 1968], when you have the bone flying in the air and a mere several tens of thousands of years later turning into a spaceship. Now we see a multiplicity of things that look like smartphones, and this makes me think of the multiplicity of images that come from those tools. Of course, this is one of the main sources of evidence that we at Forensic Architecture use. We go online, whether it's the war in Ukraine, Israeli attacks on Gaza, police violence in Chicago or in London – what is very interesting for us is those videos. If you have enough videos, spatial models become a way to synchronise and locate them. We also understand that the story is not told within each video, but between the videos. If a story is told by one video, where you have a killer and a person who gets killed in the same frame, you don't need our analysis. But if one video shows somebody running away and in

another you hear a gunshot in the background, and in yet another you see an ambulance coming – those videos don't capture the actual killing, but you have details of what happened before and after. These videos are like the aggregate earth in which the archaeological object is located, and just like in unearthing, these videos will be discarded by the kind of journalism that sieves for the trophies. Cross-referencing partial, weak signals, we try to get as close to the truth, the act of verification, as we can. We try to put as many tangents as possible across the object, and the contour slowly starts to become clear.

We've been working with such videos for ten years – day in, day out. But recently we discovered a problem: I don't think we have listened enough to what people say while they record the videos. As you know, we're very focused on the visual material. So we discussed within the team, 'OK, let's do an exercise. Shut the visual part of the screen, play the videos and just listen to what people are saying.' People are crying, shouting, praying, cursing. These speech

Detail of *Spouts*, 2015

Detail of *Untitled (Porcelain Balls)*, 2022

acts are testimonies that I call 'testimonies without memory'. They are from the moment, as things are happening, and they are incredibly important in order to understand the event from multiple perspectives.

AW
There are multiple perspectives in the film *Rashomon* [Akira Kurosawa, 1950], which has an almost philosophical conclusion. The truth we think we are dearly attached to, or believe to be solid, is imperfect. It is impossible for the truth to come from only one perspective. As humans, we are seeking the truth, but we each have a very different way of approaching it. A sound, a look, an angle or an imperfection of technology are so much richer than the truth itself. As you said, it is the environment of the situation that matters. For the exhibition, we jump from early Neolithic stones to a few thousand years later, with spouts from wine bottles from the Song dynasty [960–1279 CE]. I was at the market and I saw this object and

said, 'What is this? This is just a part of a wine bottle.' Those pieces were unearthed and found when a road got fixed, or when the ground was broken to start building something. The people who found them could easily tell what they were, because they were from an area in China that fired those materials for thousands of years. They can date them to the Song dynasty, which was a thousand years ago. Of course, at the flea markets, I would buy these things. Then something interesting started to happen. Once the sellers realised someone was buying those spouts, they started telling me, 'I have some at my home, can you wait fifteen or twenty minutes? I'll bring them to you.' I would reply, 'Yes, I will be here.' Then you'd see people coming from different directions to offer pails of spouts. They are all interested in collecting old broken objects, which have no market value because they are just fragments. Although, because they really are from that time, people think they are precious. So gradually, over years, I collected hundreds of thousands of these fragments.

Of course, they remain useless, and I think their beauty is in their uselessness. They are not functional but they show early human intention, or will, to create. They show how high the standards were, to the point that vases that were considered imperfect would be broken and buried. Again, this tells a kind of story, the will required to present a beautiful Song dynasty bottle. Nobody would ever have thought that these broken pieces would end up in a museum show. Presented together, they just look like a minimalist sculpture, in such large fields of a singular type of object. Like the *Sunflower Seeds*. They are uniform, but no two are identical. In the last few years, I found these cannonballs …

EW
… I saw those porcelain balls. I couldn't believe it …

AW
Crazy. To this day, I can't believe it. Why would they make these high-quality cannonballs, one by one? What were they thinking when they made them? None of them are the same size. They are all slightly larger or smaller, because there were no machines to make them perfectly round. Even the people who unearthed them didn't know what they were. They were found attached to the city walls.

EW
They just crashed into the wall? Into a mud wall?

AW
Yes, or they fell into the moat. They still smell like a firecracker. I shipped them to Berlin, and I wondered, 'What will customs think?' Because there is nothing like that, it used to be a weapon but isn't one any more. It's completely perfect, like a golf ball or something.

EW
I love that piece — I've seen an image of it. It struck me because I thought that porcelain was only for the most fragile things. Porcelain is what you keep, what you love. This is like a projectile, a weapon. This contradiction is a very interesting one.

AW
There's also a certain beauty to war from that time. It was not a barbarian act, but rather a challenge of who had the higher aesthetic standard. From a very early time, China had jade swords that would take years to make. You could only fight with each one once. The fact that you held it meant that your enemy would understand who you were.

EW
I was working on an archaeological site in Gaza that was being bombed by Israel. This is why I was interested in this particular site. We did a whole investigation of it, we digitally reconstructed it and we revealed what it had. I met the chief archaeologist, who is a Dominican priest. He is a very intelligent man called Jean-Baptiste Humbert, who was introduced to me by my friend Farid Armaly, a Palestinian artist. Humbert raised a precious idea, which I will never forget. Sometimes only two or three shards from a broken pot could function as 'diagnostic

Byzantine cemetery, Mission Archéologique de Gaza: Coopération Franco-Palestinienne, École Biblique et Archéologique Française, 1995–2005

Forensic Architecture, 2022. The layers of the site, ancient past to present

Forensic Architecture, 2012. Forensic anthropologist Fredy Peccerelli demonstrates the impact of a bullet fired from a gun on a skull

shards' and are enough to reconstruct the entire pot. A diagnostic shard holds within it much of the information about the entire pot. For example, it is enough to have one shard of the lip or the body to calculate the object perimeter. Archaeologists sometimes keep only two or three diagnostic shards, which hold the ghost of the whole object – like they hold the entire DNA of the object. I thought about that and Armaly's exhibition *Shar(e)d Domains* [2007] – which was beautiful – when I saw your spouts from the Song dynasty. They look like bones, right? For me, it's almost as if you are in a graveyard. However, within every bone you can reconstruct an entire life.

That is something I learned by working with forensic anthropologists in Guatemala. At that time, they were unable to do DNA analysis because it was so expensive. They would find bodies of missing people, of the indigenous Maya people who had been murdered during the military dictatorship, or of students who had disappeared, and they wanted to return them to their families. We're talking about a huge number of bodies. To identify the person from the bones, they spoke about something similar to Humbert's diagnostic-shard idea. They talked about something called osteobiography – some bones contain much information about your life: for example, what you've eaten, if you exercised, what kind of air you were breathing, from which we know if you lived high on a mountain or low. It is like an archive. This got me thinking about your *Spouts*. If you look at them in a scientific way, they are the ghost of the object. Not in a poetic sense, but you have their precise radiuses, etc.

The last thing I want to talk about, because maybe this is a very Ai Weiwei way of thinking, is how a pot breaks. I needed to learn that. I needed to understand, being in these exhumations of mass graves, what happens when a skull is shot at. A forensic anthropologist taught me that when a skull receives a bullet, the bullet is travelling two to three times the speed of sound. Cracks develop around the skull, around the bullet hole, in all directions, and they travel across to the other side of the head. However, the crack travels faster than the bullet. In other words, by the time the bullet gets to the other side of the skull, the skull is already broken. I wondered, 'How can the crack move faster than the bullet?' They explained to me that the crack is not an object, it's the void between parts of an object. This applies to pots too. If you shoot at one, you'd have one entry hole, and, because the cracks travel faster, by the time the bullet hits the back side the pot is already broken.

AW
It's interesting. This tells us that our knowledge, or common-sense understanding, is not exactly scientifically conclusive.

EW
For me, it's interesting to think about the cracks as objects. I'm thinking about the pots that you break, and the shards. We think that the crack is a non-object, like how we think of the object and the earth separately. Let's think about the crack. When buildings are destroyed by bombs, the crack finds 'the path of least resistance', the weakest part of the concrete. Let's say, fifty years

Detail of *Left Right Studio Material*, 2018

ago, somebody threw a cigarette butt into the concrete when the foundations of a building were being built. As long as the building is standing, nothing happens. When the building is destroyed, when cracks develop, they travel to that cigarette, because there the concrete is weaker. Potentially you'd also be able to see the point of cracks in the building, the irregularities in construction, the pieces of glass, the cigarette butts …

AW
You can apply that theory to politics, or judgements about the conditions of human behaviour. When I dropped the Han dynasty vases, you could call it a stupid act. It happened privately; I took a photo, I had the negative for years before I developed it. Only once people saw it did the vase start to break. Depending on whether it was seen as real or fake, it was judged differently. Because our whole system is structured on our judgement of value, on what we care about. That also goes for larger political movements. People die for different reasons: a boat capsizes or there is a car crash, for example. In the past ten days, if you counted them, there could be hundreds or thousands of people dead. So why should one

life be valued more highly than another? Why does one situation draw the public's emotions more than another? It is worth studying that. To see why our emotions are so strong in some cases, but in other cases someone's death doesn't really affect us. As you asked, 'What is our weak point that transmits all the cracks?' I think that this could be interesting to study, not just for physical or scientific conclusions, but to understand human behaviour or society. What structures our mental condition? Education? Money? Power? Safety? Your story is very interesting.

I have another work made from fragments left after I had two studios destroyed by the authorities. It made no sense — why did they have to do it? They acted with no explanation. They don't care whether you understand or not. They might not even understand, but it happens anyway. That can also be compared to many things — on a personal scale, like an argument between a husband and wife, or on a larger scale, like wars between two nations. Each results in a different reality. The building has collapsed, and the porcelain is broken or shattered. It remains as evidence. Evidence is such a beautiful word because it doesn't take sides. ○

we

Maki

Biographies

Brian Dillon is a writer and curator based in London. He is currently professor of Creative Writing at Queen Mary, University of London. His writings have appeared in the *Guardian* and the *New Yorker*, among others. He has curated exhibitions for Tate and the Hayward Gallery.

Rachel Hajek is a curator, writer and researcher based in London. She is assistant curator at the Design Museum where she has contributed to numerous exhibitions and displays, and has previously held positions at Tate Modern.

Julia Lovell is a scholar, prize-winning author and translator focusing on China. She is professor of Modern Chinese History and Literature at Birkbeck, University of London. She is the author of many books, including *The Opium War: Drugs, Dreams and the Making of China* (2011); *Splendidly Fantastic: Architecture and Power Games in China* (2012); and *Maoism: A Global History* (2019).

Tim Marlow is a writer, broadcaster and art historian. He is the chief executive and director of the Design Museum in London. Prior to this role, he was the artistic director of the Royal Academy of Arts in London. He has lectured on art and culture in over forty countries.

Justin McGuirk is a writer and curator based in London. He is the chief curator at the Design Museum and the director of Future Observatory, a national programme for design research supporting the green transition.

Wang Shu is a Chinese architect based in Hangzhou, China. He is the dean of the School of Architecture of the China Academy of Art. Together with his partner, Lu Wenyu, he founded the firm Amateur Architecture Studio.

Eyal Weizman is a British-Israeli architect. He is the director of the research agency Forensic Architecture. He is also professor of Spatial and Visual Cultures and a founding director of the Centre for Research Architecture at the Department of Visual Cultures, Goldsmiths, University of London.

Index

Page numbers in *italics* refer to illustrations and information contained in captions.

Picture Credits

Every reasonable attempt has been made to identify owners of copyright. Errors and omissions notified to the publisher will be corrected in subsequent editions. Abbreviations are: T – top, B – bottom, L – left, R – right.

Unless otherwise stated all images are © Courtesy Ai Weiwei Studio.

Acknowledgements

This book was published in conjunction with the exhibition *Ai Weiwei: Making Sense* at the Design Museum, London, 7 April to 30 July 2023.

The exhibition was organised in collaboration with Ai Weiwei.

Chief Curator
Justin McGuirk

Assistant Curator
Rachel Hajek

Exhibitions Project Managers
Cassandra Needham
Cleo Stringer

Public Realm Project Manager
Rebecca Gremmo

Exhibitions Coordinator
Giulia Cozzi

Graphic Design
Twelve

3D Design Support
All Things Studio

Curatorial Research Volunteers
Chloe Fujimoto
Yichen Lu

The Design Museum would like to thank Ai Weiwei Studio: Yun-hua Chen, Cui Xing, Gui Nuo, Li Dongxu, Jennifer Ng, Nadine Stenke, Sun Mo, Kimberly Sung, Xia Xing, Xu Ye and Chin-Chin Yap.

With additional thanks from the Design Museum and Ai Weiwei to Lisson Gallery, Wang Fen, maybe art, Mao Ran, Galleria Continua and David Adamson.

PRINCIPAL FUNDER

⓫ REUBEN FOUNDATION

EXHIBITION SPONSOR

With additional support from the Ai Weiwei Supporters Circle:
David and Debbie Stileman, Bianca and Stuart Roden, John Burbank,
Anne-Lindsay Makepeace and Tarun Jotwani.

Design Museum Publishing
Design Museum Enterprises Ltd
224–238 Kensington High Street
London W8 6AG
United Kingdom

First published in 2023
© 2023 Design Museum Publishing

978-1-872005-63-8

Publishing Manager
Mark Cortes Favis

Editor
Justin McGuirk

Assistant Editor
Rachel Hajek

Editorial Assistant
Stefano Mancin

Picture Researcher
Anabel Navarro

Copyeditor
Simon Coppock

Proofreaders
Ian McDonald
Cecilia Tricker

Indexer
Nic Nicholas

Graphic Designers
Twelve with Mark Cortes Favis

Design Museum Publishing would like to thank
Yun-hua Chen and Kimberly Sung at Ai Weiwei
Studio; Rob Squires, Stewart Bennett and Sam
Adams at Pureprint; Shi Yuan, Marco Minzoni
and Johanna Currie at Twelve; photographer
Michael Radford; as well as Siobhán Tighe,
Kirsty West and many other colleagues at
the Design Museum who have supported this
exhibition catalogue.

The body text in this catalogue is typeset in
Song Ti. Designed by Sinotype in the 1990s, it
was the first digital typeface to be widely used
in Chinese. It was inspired by Bembo Infant, a
Renaissance type used frequently in children's
books. The typeface for the catalogue and
chapter titles is a unicase font designed by
Thomas Huot-Marchand.

Distribution
UK, Europe and select territories around
the world
Thames & Hudson
181A High Holborn
London WC1V 7QX
United Kingdom
thamesandhudson.com

USA and Canada
ARTBOOK | D.A.P.
75 Broad Street, Suite 630
New York, NY 10004
United States of America
artbook.com

Printed and bound in the UK by Pureprint

Cover image
The artist's hand holding one of the Neolithic tools, 2023